AR level 7.7

P9-DEV-552

DISCARDED

MARTIN LUTHER KING, JR.

"We Shall Overcome"

Anne Schraff

Kaneland Middle School
1N137 Meredith Rd.
Maple Park, IL 60151

Series Consultant:
Dr. Russell L. Adams, Chairman
Department of
Afro-American Studies,
Howard University

Enslow Publishers, Inc.

40 Industrial Road	PO Box 38
Box 398	Aldershot
Berkeley Heights, NJ 07922	Hants GU12 6BP
USA	UK

http://www.enslow.com

"I STILL BELIEVE THAT WE SHALL OVERCOME."
—Martin Luther King, Jr.
December 10, 1964

Copyright © 2005 by Anne Schraff

All rights reserved.

No part of this book may be reproduced by any means
without the written permission of the publisher.

Library of Congress Cataloging-in-Publication Data

Schraff, Anne E.
    Martin Luther King Jr. : "we shall overcome" / Anne Schraff.
      p. cm. — (African-American biography library)
    Includes bibliographical references and index.
    ISBN-10: 0-7660-1774-5
    1. King, Martin Luther, Jr., 1929–1968—Juvenile literature. 2. African Americans—
Biography—Juvenile literature. 3. Civil rights workers—United States—Biography—
Juvenile literature 4. Baptists—United States—Clergy—Biography—Juvenile literature.
5. African Americans—Civil rights—History—20th century—Juvenile literature. I. Title.
II. Series.
    E185.97.K5S365 2005
    323'.092—dc22

                                 2004027542

ISBN-13: 978-0-7660-1774-0

Printed in the United States of America

10 9 8 7 6 5 4 3 2

To Our Readers:
We have done our best to make sure all Internet Addresses in this book were active and appropriate when we went to press. However, the author and the publisher have no control over and
assume no liability for the material available on those Internet sites or on other Web sites they
may link to. Any comments or suggestions can be sent by e-mail to comments@enslow.com or
to the address on the back cover.

Every effort has been made to locate all copyright holders of material used in this book. If any
errors or omissions have occurred, corrections will be made in future editions of this book.

Illustration Credits: AP Photo/Curtis Compton, p. 107; AP/Wide World, pp. 3, 4 (portrait),
7, 12, 23, 29, 33, 38 (both), 41, 43, 47, 52, 53, 55, 57, 59, 63, 65 (both), 69, 73, 76, 78, 80, 82,
85, 87, 90, 93, 97, 101, 102, 104, 111; D.C. Public Library, p. 31; Library of Congress, p. 18;
Morehouse College, p. 25; National Archives and Records Administration, p. 45; National Park
Service (National Historic Site), p. 14.

Cover Illustrations: AP/Wide World.

Contents

We Shall Overcome

"I've Had Enough"

T he twenty-nine-year-old African-American Baptist minister, Martin Luther King, Jr., walked toward the Montgomery County Courthouse with his wife, Coretta, and their friend the Reverend Ralph Abernathy. It was September 3, 1958. On this day, a man who had attacked Abernathy in his church office was going on trial. The Kings had come along to support Abernathy.

As they neared the courthouse door, a white guard shouted at King that since he had no business here, he should stay out. King asked if he could speak with his friend's lawyer. Two white police officers appeared. "Boy, you done done it," one of the officers yelled at King. "Let's go."[1] Startled, King did not move. The police officer jerked King's arm behind his back and started dragging him away. The officers roughly pulled him down the sidewalk and around the corner to the police station.

Coretta King watched in horror as her husband was hauled down the street. As she ran after him, one of the officers turned and snapped, "Gal, you want to go too? Just nod your head."[2]

King cautioned his wife to say nothing. The couple had two small children at home. King was being arrested. If his wife also ended up in jail, there would be nobody to care for the children. So Coretta King remained silent.

King was taken before the desk sergeant at the police station. The sergeant took one look at the young minister and ordered him locked up. King was hustled down a dark corridor to a cell door. He was frisked for weapons. Then one of the officers grabbed King by the throat, choking him before flinging him into the cell and slamming the door.

Martin Luther King, Jr., was well known in the United States as a civil rights leader. But the police officers who treated him so roughly did not know who they were dealing with. Nor did they notice the photographer on the street taking pictures of the brutal arrest.

When Montgomery authorities realized they had arrested Martin Luther King, Jr., they quickly released him. He was told he would be charged only with failure to obey an officer. That night King told his wife, "I've had enough."[3] He was tired of the way black people were routinely mistreated by the law. He decided not to pay his fine and to go to jail instead as a protest.

Ralph Abernathy, left, and Martin Luther King, Jr.

When King was tried and convicted, he was fined $10 or fourteen days in jail. King declared to the court that he would not pay a fine "for an act that I did not commit and above all for brutal treatment that I did not deserve."[4] Fearing more bad publicity, the officials of Montgomery County paid King's fine.

Martin Luther King, Jr., would see the insides of many more jail cells and courtrooms in his struggle to, as he put it that day, "wipe out the scourge of brutality and violence inflicted upon Negroes who seek only to walk with dignity before God and Man."[5]

Chapter 2

"The Perfect Child"

Martin Luther King, Jr., was born January 15, 1929, in Atlanta, Georgia, and named after his father. His father's nickname was Mike, and the baby's birth certificate said "Michael," not Martin. The error was not noticed until a few years later.

The Kings called their new baby M.L. He was so serene at birth that the doctor had to spank him several times to get him to utter his first cry.

M.L. was born into a strong Baptist tradition. His mother, Alberta Williams King, was the daughter of the Reverend Adam Daniel Williams, pastor of Ebenezer Baptist Church in Atlanta. M.L.'s father was assistant pastor at the same church.

"From the very beginning I was an extraordinarily healthy child. . . . The doctors pronounced me a 100 percent perfect child."[1]

M.L.'s father, the Reverend Mike King, was a strong, tough-minded man. Born on a sharecropping farm in central Georgia, he had spent his youth working the fields with a plow driven by a mule. As a boy, his first chore every morning was to groom the mule, brushing the animal's coat. Teased that he was beginning to smell like a mule, the teenager declared defiantly, "I don't think like a mule."[2]

Mike had a difficult childhood, as his father was an alcoholic. When he was just fifteen, Mike intervened to protect his mother from his father's drunken rages.

Early in his life, Mike saw white people abusing blacks. One day, when he failed to move fast enough to bring water to a white employer, he too was struck. Mike worked at many jobs, including helping a mechanic in a repair shop, but he was always fascinated by the emotional preachers at the Baptist pulpit. He felt called to the ministry, so he struggled to pay for the education that would open that door for him. After he earned a college degree in religion, he became a Baptist preacher.

M.L.'s mother, Alberta Williams, had grown up with a comfortable life as the daughter of a pastor and received a good education. In the early 1920s, Mike King began dating Alberta, taking her for drives in his

Sharecropping

When slavery ended, many black men became sharecroppers. The men rented small plots of land, but they had no money for seeds, equipment, or even food. The owner of the farm provided what they needed in exchange for a share of the profits when the crops came in.

Model T Ford. She was a shy young woman, and Mike had a strong, dynamic personality. The couple married on Thanksgiving Day in 1926. They moved into the upstairs of Alberta's parents' twelve-room house. Mike King became the assistant pastor in his father-in-law's church.

A daughter, Christine, was born to the family, followed a year later by the birth of M.L. The third and last child was Alfred Daniel. The King children enjoyed a happy life in the large house on Auburn Avenue. M.L. called it "a very congenial home situation," in a family where "love was central."[3]

The Kings lived in a pleasant middle-class African-American neighborhood. M.L. was an active, athletic boy who enjoyed playing basketball with his friends in the large vacant lot behind his house. He flew kites, made model airplanes, and rode his bicycle through the streets. A favorite indoor activity was sliding down the banister of the two-story Victorian house. Once, when M.L. leaned too hard on the banister, he went flying twenty-five feet, bouncing through an open door into the cellar. Remarkably, he came out of the fall unhurt.

M.L. later praised his father as "a real father," who "always put his family first."[4] He called him "Daddy," and said he was "as strong in his will as he is in his body."[5] Mike King was muscular, weighing more than two hundred pounds. M.L. called his mother Mother Dear. She was a short, quiet woman who rarely lost her temper. She

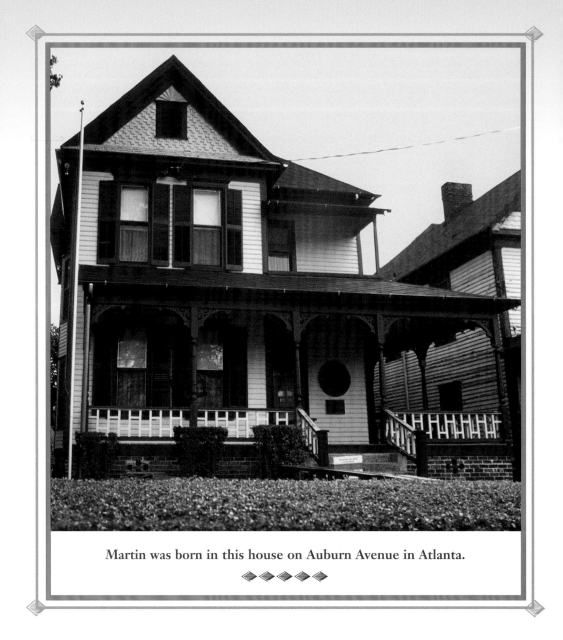

Martin was born in this house on Auburn Avenue in Atlanta.

dressed nicely and had a friendly smile and a warm greeting for everyone.

The relative who held an extra special place in M.L.'s heart was his mother's mother, Grandmother Williams. M.L. later called her a "saintly grandmother."[6] She told the children Bible stories, and M.L. felt that he was her favorite.

In the spring of 1931, Reverend Adam Daniel Williams died, and M.L.'s father became pastor of Ebenezer Baptist Church. He increased church membership and renovated the church building. By the mid-1930s, Mike King was a respected African-American leader in Atlanta. He had joined the National Association for the Advancement of Colored People (NAACP), and he was ready to challenge the evils of segregation. He preached about black voters' rights at a time when only whites could vote. In 1935, he led one thousand blacks in a voter registration drive. He also campaigned successfully for equal pay for black teachers.

One day when M.L. was small, he was out with his father when a police officer pulled the car over for driving past a stop sign. The white officer called out, "All right, boy, pull over and let me see your license. M.L.'s father pointed to his son beside him and said, "This is a boy. I'm a man, and until you call me one, I will not listen to you."[7] The officer wrote the ticket and left.

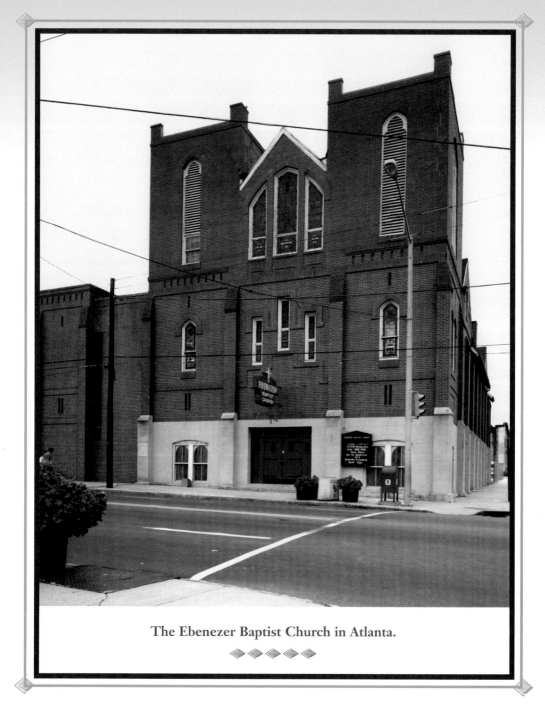

The Ebenezer Baptist Church in Atlanta.

Young M.L. had an incredible memory. By the age of five he could recite entire Bible passages and sing hymns using all the correct words. M.L. was so smart that his parents sent him to school a year early. When M.L. was asked his age, he truthfully said he was five. The school sent him home with instructions to his parents to wait a year before sending him back. The school was not for five-year-olds.

At age six, M.L. started singing in church groups, accompanied by his mother on the piano. He was an instant celebrity, performing emotional gospel songs with great fervor. He often sang "I Want to Be More and More Like Jesus."[8] To see the small boy expressing such sincere faith caused some of the congregation to weep and cry out in joy.

M.L.'s father had grown up in grim poverty, and he wanted better lives for his own children. He prayed daily that his children would have an easier time than he had. Mike King was very strict with money, and he ran the house with firm rules. The children always got what they needed, but for extras like ice cream and sodas, they had to spend their allowances. M.L.'s father assigned tasks to the children and praised them for jobs well done. In the King house there was one authority: Daddy King. Neither his wife nor his mother-in-law, Grandma Williams, ever questioned that fact.

When M.L. or his sister or brother misbehaved, there was surely a punishment. The children did not dare act rude or sassy lest their father strap them. Sometimes he made the children whip each other for misdeeds. Most of all, M.L. hated to disappoint his father. Letting his father down hurt M.L. more than the whipping that would surely follow.

One time when Alfred Daniel, known as A.D., was teasing his sister, Christine, M.L. became so upset that he hit his brother with the telephone. Alfred was knocked out by the impact. Daddy King punished M.L. for this act of violence, whipping him until tears flowed from the boy's eyes. Even so, M.L. did not object. He took the punishment in silence. Grandma Williams, however, was so distraught to see him whipped so hard that she rushed from the room crying. But she did not try to stop M.L.'s father from punishing the boy.

M.L. knew that whenever he was punished, it hurt his grandmother, and that fact made him love her dearly. One day when the boys were playing, A.D. slid down the banister and accidentally kicked Grandma Williams, who was standing at the bottom of the stairs. The elderly lady fell to the floor and did not move. M.L. ran to his grandmother and stared down at her in fear. He thought she had been killed by the accident. He felt guilty that his reckless play with his brother had caused the death of his beloved grandmother. M.L. was so guilt-ridden and heartbroken that he ran up to his room and threw himself from the open window, dropping twelve feet to the earth below.

M.L. lay there as his relatives, including Grandma Williams, now up and feeling fine, hurried to his side. When M.L. heard his grandmother's voice calling to him, he got to his feet, unhurt.

M.L.'s best friend in early childhood was a white boy whose father owned a store across the street. In September 1935, the two six-year-olds started school. M.L. went to the school for black children, and his friend went to the whites-only school. M.L. expected that they would still get together after school, and he was deeply hurt when the white boy said their friendship was over. The boy's mother would not let them play anymore.

Traditionally at that time in the South, white and black children could be close friends when they were very young, but as they came of school age the relationships had to end. In later years, M.L. would recall the loss of his friend as one of the most painful experiences of his childhood. "I never will forget what a great shock this was to me," he said.[9] M.L. was so troubled that he struggled with feelings of hatred toward white people. When he talked to his parents about it, they told him it was his Christian duty to love white people. The boy asked himself, "How could I love a race of people who hated me and who had been responsible for breaking me up with one of my best childhood friends?"[10]

On the heels of losing his friend, M.L. went downtown with his father for a new pair of shoes. When Daddy

Martin was just a little boy when he learned about the grim realities of segregation.

◆ ◆ ◆ ◆

King sat down to help his son try on some shoes, a white clerk hurried over to tell them to go to the rear of the store. African Americans were not allowed to shop in the main part of the store, he said. M.L.'s father angrily left without buying anything.

M.L. was living in a strictly segregated Atlanta, and he soon became aware of all the restrictions on African Americans. They could not use the public parks or eat inside the restaurants. They were welcome at just one black theater, where the movies were all years old. At age eight, when M.L. accidentally stepped on a white woman's foot, she slapped him across the face and insulted him. One day, after seeing a brutal attack on a black passenger, M.L.'s father refused to ride the segregated city buses anymore. Daddy King said, "I don't care how long I have to live with this system, I will never accept it."[11]

On May 18, 1941, twelve-year-old M.L. sneaked out to watch a parade without his parents' permission. He was enjoying the colorful marching bands when someone he knew rushed up to tell him that something terrible had happened to Grandmother Williams at home. M.L. had thought she was at church, and he ran home, his heart pounding with fear. There, he learned that his grandmother had suffered a heart attack and died on the way to the hospital.

Once more, M.L. was stricken with sorrow and guilt. He asked himself why God had allowed such a thing to happen. Why had God taken his grandmother, the person he loved most in the world? In his tortured mind, M.L. believed that God was punishing him for his disobedience in going to the parade without his parents' knowledge.

The boy could not bear the torment he felt. He rushed up to his room and once again hurled himself through the open window. His body smacked the ground below. As he lay bruised and trembling, his parents rushed to his side. He was not seriously hurt, but for many days he stayed in his room, crying. M.L.'s father tried to soothe him, explaining that God took people whenever He was ready for them, and it had nothing to do with anything M.L. had done.

Growing up in a deeply religious family, M.L. had always believed that when good people die they go to heaven, where they are reunited with their loved ones. The death of his grandmother affected him so profoundly that from that day on, his belief in life after death was unshakable. Years later, referring to the death of his grandmother, he said, "This is why today I am such a strong believer in personal immortality."[12]

Not long after the death of Grandma Williams, the King family moved to a two-story brick house in a better neighborhood. The children were growing into their teens. Christine was very obedient, A.D. was sometimes rebellious, and M.L. could be obedient at times and rebellious at others. He continued to get whippings from his father until he was fifteen years old.

As a teenager, M.L. outwrestled his friends, played the piano, and enjoyed opera. He was a student at Booker T. Washington High School, and learning came easily to him. He loved to read and was always in the middle of a book. He also enjoyed eating soul food, especially fried chicken, cornbread, collard greens, ham hocks, and bacon drippings. M.L. struggled with conflicting feelings about his father. He loved and respected his father, but he wanted to be independent, too. He felt certain that he never wanted to follow in his father's footsteps and become a minister.

In the eleventh grade, M.L. entered an oratorical contest. His topic was "The Negro and the Constitution." M.L. won a prize for his speech, and he was in high spirits riding home on the bus from Dublin, Georgia, to Atlanta. At a stop along the way, some white passengers boarded the bus. There were not enough empty seats, so the white driver ordered the black students to get up and give their seats to the white newcomers. M.L. wanted to defy the order, but his teacher, Mrs. Bradley, whom he respected, persuaded him to move. For the next ninety miles to Atlanta, M.L. and the other black students had to stand in the aisle. King later said, "It was the angriest I have ever been in my life."[13]

In the spring of 1944, fifteen-year-old M.L. passed a special examination for early admittance to Atlanta's Morehouse College. That summer, Morehouse sponsored him for a job at a tobacco farm in Connecticut. M.L. had delivered newspapers since age eleven, but this would be his first real job. The fact that it was many miles from home appealed to the restless teenager. He was getting away for the first time in his life.

> M.L. loved to read books about black history and heroic African Americans.

Even though the job entailed long hours working with tobacco plants in the hot sun, M.L. enjoyed it very much. On weekends he went into the nearby town of Hartford, where he had his first taste of integration. He spoke of an "exhilarating sense of freedom."[14] In a June 1944 letter to his father, he wrote, "The white people here are very nice. We go to any place we want to and sit anywhere we want to."[15]

Young Martin Luther King, Jr., was getting his first glimpse of an integrated world. He would later devote his life to trying to make this a reality all over America.

Chapter 3

Minister and Husband

Martin Luther King, Jr., skipped his final year at Booker T. Washington High School to enter the freshman class at Morehouse College in September 1944. He had no clear idea of what he wanted to do with his life. He considered being a doctor or a lawyer, or even getting into politics. While a student at Morehouse, he lived at home and commuted to his classes. He dated young women from Spelman and Clark colleges, and he joined the Morehouse football team and glee club.

King finally chose sociology as his major, and English as his minor. To his distress, he discovered that his schooling had not prepared him well for college-level work. He was reading at just an eighth-grade level, and the teachers at Morehouse demanded much more than that. It became painfully clear to King that the black schools he had

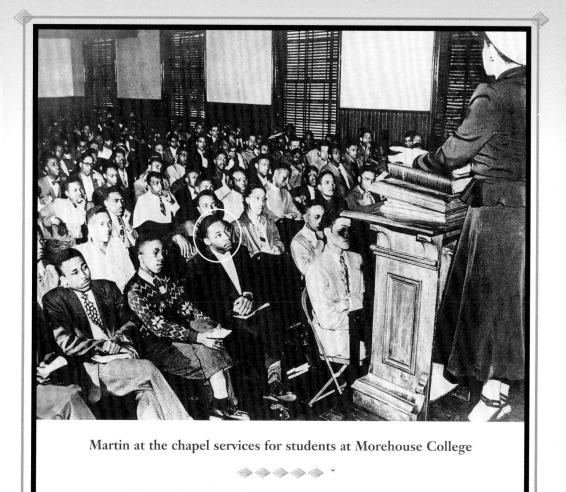

Martin at the chapel services for students at Morehouse College

attended in Atlanta were not good enough. They did not fully prepare their students to succeed in college. King's English teacher at Morehouse gave him a C-plus, but commented that "he would have had an A based just on interest."[1]

King's professors at Morehouse described modern clergymen as rational beings, spiritually and intellectually

Sociology

Sociology, which Martin studied in college, is the study of human behavior as people interact with each other. Sociologists try to find out how human relationships work. They try to understand why people act the way they do and how to help people live and work together successfully.

strong, determined to help make people's lives better. This depiction appealed to King, and he opened his mind to the possibility of entering the ministry. At the age of seventeen, he made the decision to become a Baptist minister. He said later of that moment, "I came to see that God had placed a responsibility upon my shoulders."[2]

When King told his father of his decision, the senior King was delighted but did not reveal this to his son. Instead, he suggested that the young man preach a trial sermon in one of the smaller auditoriums in Ebenezer Baptist Church. When Martin Luther King, Jr., began preaching, his sermon drew so many people that they had to move the service to the main auditorium. Daddy King felt grateful to have such a son.[3]

In 1947, eighteen-year-old Martin Luther King, Jr., was appointed assistant pastor of Ebenezer Baptist Church. In the summers he worked as a laborer on the railroad, loading and unloading trains in Atlanta's suffocating heat. There, he was among a class of black people he had never met before—the hardworking black poor. For King, it was a glimpse into another world.

In the spring of 1948, King graduated from Morehouse College with a degree in sociology. He decided to pursue his divinity degree at Crozer Theological Seminary. King longed to be his own man, and the college in Chester, Pennsylvania, on the banks of the Delaware River, seemed an ideal place for stepping outside his father's large shadow.

Crozer Seminary had one hundred students, including twelve women and six blacks. For the first time in his life,

In college, Martin played football and sang in the glee club.

King was in a mostly white school, competing with the brightest students. He got A's in all his subjects. His time at Morehouse College had erased the gap in his education from Atlanta's segregated school system.

Living among whites was a new experience for King. Once, when a student at Crozer had his room vandalized, he blamed King. This student was known for his bigoted attitude toward blacks. He rushed to King's room in a rage and threatened to shoot him. King remained calm as he quietly assured the young man that he was not the vandal. Later, King refused to press charges against this student for his violent threats. The student eventually apologized for the false accusation. The other white students respected King greatly for his spirit of forgiveness.[4]

It was at Crozer that Martin Luther King, Jr., began seriously studying nonviolence as a philosophy. At first he believed that war could be a "negative good in stopping the spread of an evil."[5] Then he attended a lecture given by Mordecai Johnson, president of Howard University, in Washington, D.C., on the life of Mohandas K. Gandhi of India. King later described being "electrified" by Gandhi's philosophy.[6] He read six books on Gandhi's life and embraced the idea that love had the power to overcome all evil. King now believed that doing nothing in the face of evil was cowardly, but confronting it nonviolently was the height of courage. He decided to live by the principle that nonviolent action would lead to "the creation of the

◆◆◆◆◆◆◆◆◆◆◆◆◆◆◆◆◆◆◆◆◆◆◆◆◆◆◆◆◆◆◆◆

"Mahatma" (Great Soul) Gandhi

Mohandas Gandhi was India's greatest spiritual and political leader. For more than forty years, he used fasting, peaceful resistance, and boycotts to lead the people of India to freedom from British rule. He frequently used nonviolent demonstrations to fight unjust laws and the unfair treatment of certain groups in India. He was assassinated in 1948, the year after he negotiated independence for his country.

beloved community," while the "aftermath of violence is tragic bitterness."[7]

In June 1951, King was awarded a degree in divinity, graduating at the top of his class. He also received a $1,300 scholarship for graduate school. He decided to attend Boston University's prestigious School of Theology, where he would pursue his Ph.D.—the highest university degree—in systematic theology.

After a summer in Atlanta, King drove to Boston in his brand-new green Chevrolet, a gift from his father. He had a problem finding a place to live in the city. He went to many places that advertised rooms for rent—but "they were for rent until they found out I was a Negro, and suddenly they had just been rented," he said.[8] Eventually, he did find a room.

King joined the lively social life of Boston, frequenting

the Western Lunch Box, which served the kind of southern food he was used to. At night, he and his friends enjoyed hot jazz at the Totem Pole. Though he dated many young women, King could not find that one special person he might want to settle down with. One day, while having lunch with a married friend, Mary Powell, a student at the New England Conservatory of Music in Boston, King asked, "Do you know any nice, attractive young ladies?"[9]

Powell mentioned Coretta Scott, a fellow student at the conservatory, whom she described as "pretty and intelligent."[10] King called Scott at home, introducing himself as a friend of Mary Powell's. He said he had heard "wonderful things" about her. Could he take her to lunch?[11] Scott agreed to the lunch date, and King promised to pick her up at the conservatory in his green Chevrolet. He told her the trip usually took ten minutes, but he was so eager to meet her, he would make it in seven minutes.[12]

Scott and King lunched in a cafeteria with cold rain pouring down outside. Later, Scott recalled her first impressions of King. "How short he seems, how unimpressive," she thought.[13] But as King talked, Scott found that "he radiated so much charm" that he became "much better looking."[14] As for King, his first impression of Coretta Scott was very favorable. He liked her hair, her shy, pretty smile, and her personality.[15] They talked for a long time, and as King was driving Scott back to the

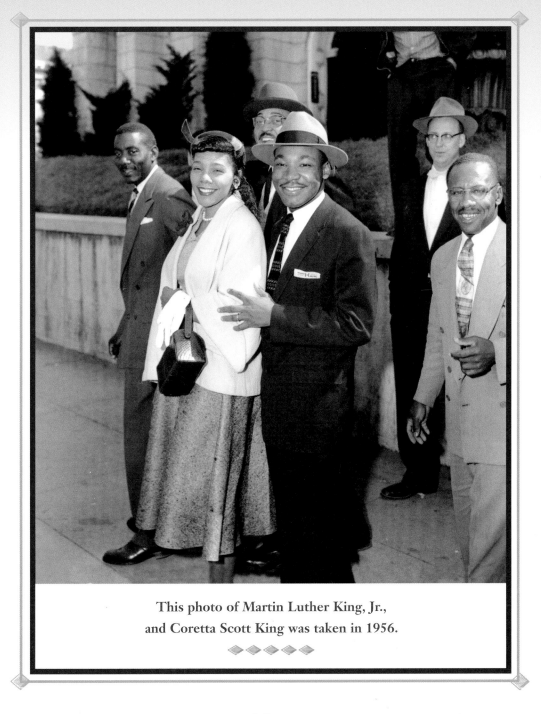

This photo of Martin Luther King, Jr.,
and Coretta Scott King was taken in 1956.

conservatory, he said, "Do you know what? You have everything I have ever wanted in a wife." He then named the qualities that attracted him: "character, intelligence, personality, and beauty."[16] Scott was astonished by the comment, but agreed to let him call her again.

Coretta Scott's economic background differed from King's. She was born on a farm in rural Marion, Alabama. Over the years, her hardworking parents had managed to create a comfortable life for their family. Scott gained an education through scholarships, graduating from Antioch College in 1951 with a degree in music and education. She had a lovely mezzo-soprano voice. She hoped for a musical career and was in no rush to get married. She also had a distaste for Baptist preachers, believing them to be narrow-minded, overly pious people.[17]

At a party they both attended in suburban Watertown, Massachusetts, Coretta Scott noticed that other women were attracted to Martin Luther King, Jr. This impressed her, and she accepted more dates with him. The young couple walked together along the ocean and went to concerts in Boston's Symphony Hall. They ice-skated and shared their philosophies of life. King told Scott that he wanted to help humanity. He also frankly admitted that he saw the role of a wife as homemaker and mother. Scott realized that any dreams of a musical career would end if she married King.

Martin and Coretta, seated, posed for a portrait with
his parents, left; sister Willie Christine; and brother A.D.

> King said
> he was
> attracted
> to Coretta
> Scott's
> "character,
> intelligence,
> personality,
> and beauty."

As the dating grew more serious, King introduced Scott to his family. After some initial stress, Daddy King approved the union. In June 1953, twenty-four-year-old Martin Luther King, Jr., and his family, traveling in a motorcade, pulled up at the Scott home in Marion, Alabama. The Scotts all liked King, and on June 18, Daddy King performed the marriage ceremony for the couple on the lawn. King's younger brother, A.D., was best man.

Because there were no bridal suites available in the area—none of the local hotels would accommodate blacks—Coretta and Martin spent their wedding night in the home of a friend, who was a funeral director. "Do you know," King often joked, "we spent our honeymoon at a funeral parlor?"[18]

Back in Boston, the newlyweds rented a four-room apartment and resumed their studies. In June 1954, Coretta Scott King would graduate from the conservatory. While she was busy studying, King was a real helpmate. He cleaned the apartment, washed the clothes, and hung them to dry in the kitchen. He cooked, too, often preparing his favorite dish—cabbage, pork chops, and pigs' feet.

Like his father, King was very thrifty. He kept a three-ring notebook in which he listed all family expenses. He recorded every purchase, no matter how small. In the summer of 1953, he was working on his doctoral thesis, along with doing the housework. A thesis is a long, detailed research paper required to earn a Ph.D. The young couple was short of money, and King knew he needed to find employment as a minister soon.

King received an offer to become pastor of Dexter Avenue Baptist Church in Montgomery, Alabama. This was the church attended by many black professors at Alabama

Dexter Avenue Baptist Church in Montgomery, Alabama.

❖ ❖ ❖ ❖ ❖

State University, as well as other black professionals. King flew there in January 1954 to deliver a trial sermon. It would give the congregation an opportunity to see if the prospective minister would fit in. The congregation loved the young minister and his sermon. King was offered the job at $4,300 a year. the highest salary paid to a black minister in Montgomery, Alabama.

When King told his wife about his warm reception in Alabama, she had mixed feelings. She, like her husband, enjoyed the integrated atmosphere of Boston. She recalled the harsh segregation of her youth, and she dreaded returning to the South. Complicating the decision was Daddy King's offer for his son to become associate pastor at Ebenezer Baptist Church in Atlanta.

Martin Luther King, Jr., urged his wife to take a look at Dexter Avenue Baptist Church before they made their decision. In Alabama, Coretta King was depressed to see black people riding in the backs of buses and the general oppression of the black community. She shuddered at the thought of bringing up their children in that atmosphere. But she told her husband, "If this is what you want, I'll make myself happy in Montgomery."[19]

Chapter 4

The Responsibility of Leadership

In March 1954, when the Kings moved to Montgomery, Martin Luther King, Jr., was still working on his doctorate. He commuted back and forth to Boston to finish his work. He was awarded his Ph.D., or doctorate, in divinity on June 1955. Now he was ready to focus completely on his job in the spacious, slightly run-down parsonage of Dexter Avenue Baptist Church. King threw himself energetically into his work as pastor, rising at five-thirty each morning. He visited the sick and shut-in parishioners, conducted five to ten meetings a week, and spent fifteen hours a week writing his Sunday sermons.

On November 17, 1955, the Kings celebrated the birth of their first child, Yolanda Denise, nicknamed Yoki.

King said that she "was a big little girl—she weighed nine pounds and eleven ounces. She kept her father quite busy walking the floor."[1]

In the mid-1950s, Montgomery, like most Southern cities, was strictly segregated. In 1954, the Supreme Court had ruled in *Brown* v. *Board of Education* that having separate schools for blacks and whites was unconstitutional. This gave African Americans hope that the walls of segregation were beginning to crumble. A sore point in Montgomery was the bus system. The majority of riders were black, but seating on the city buses was segregated—with black people forced to sit in the back. They were often treated rudely by drivers.

On December 1, 1955, Rosa Parks, a black seamstress and NAACP secretary, was taking her usual ride home after a long day at work. The seats in the white section of the bus were all filled, and more white passengers boarded the bus. The driver walked down the aisle and told Parks and some other black riders to yield their seats to the white passengers who had just arrived. Parks politely refused. As a result, the police were called and Parks was taken to jail.

The arrest of the soft-spoken, well-respected Rosa Parks energized the civil rights movement in Montgomery. Martin Luther King, Jr., and an outspoken young black minister named Ralph Abernathy, attended a meeting of religious leaders to discuss what to do. They decided to boycott the Montgomery bus system and demand that its twenty thousand black riders be treated more fairly. A one-day bus boycott was planned for December 5, the same day Rosa Parks was scheduled to be tried for refusing to give up her seat.

On the morning of the boycott, there was great tension in the black community. The Kings waited anxiously to see if the African Americans of Montgomery would unite to avoid riding the buses. Many of them would have to walk long distances or find rides with the lucky few who owned cars. The winter weather was chilly and often rainy. King was not sure that so many weary, working people would be ready to make the sacrifice.

At 6 A.M. Coretta King, who had been watching from the front window of their home, cried, "Martin! Martin! Come quickly." King joined his wife at the window to see the first bus of the South Jackson line rolling by. Pointing to the bus, Coretta King said, "Darling, it's empty!"[2] The Kings counted eight black passengers all morning on buses that were usually packed with black riders. During the day it was the same—the boycott was a huge success.

Rosa Parks went to court and was convicted of violating the Alabama desegregation law. She was ordered to pay a fine of $10, plus $4 in court costs. That was exactly what the civil rights leaders had hoped would happen. Now they could challenge Parks's conviction in the courts

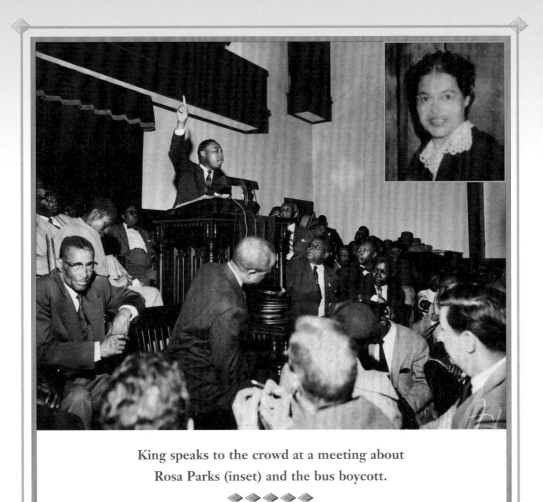

King speaks to the crowd at a meeting about
Rosa Parks (inset) and the bus boycott.

❖ ❖ ❖ ❖ ❖

and try to use the legal system to overturn bus segregation as unconstitutional.

A group of Montgomery ministers formed the Montgomery Improvement Association (MIA), and King was elected president. The boycott continued past the first day, and the MIA made its mission known. It demanded that black bus drivers be hired for routes that were mostly black; that seating be handled on a first come, first served basis; and that black passengers be treated with courtesy. As leader of the MIA, King spoke eloquently to his followers, telling them to "protest courageously, and yet with dignity and Christian love."[3] The congregation greeted King's call with thunderous applause. For months to come, 95 percent of the black riders of Montgomery would boycott the buses.

Volunteers were organized by the MIA to answer phones and coordinate rides with a fleet of 150 private cars, carpools, and black taxis, which lowered their rates. The volunteers ran a public and private transportation system.[4] King later said that he was so busy, he hardly had "time to breathe."[5]

A hectic schedule was not the only price King paid for leading the boycott. He was harassed and threatened. He was arrested in Montgomery for driving thirty miles per hour in a twenty-five-mile-per-hour zone, and he was placed in a jail cell with drunks and serious criminals. When hundreds of angry African Americans surrounded the jail, King was released with the promise that he would appear for his trial.

Threats and hate mail arrived daily at the parsonage. King worried that something would happen to him and that his followers would react with violence. He pleaded with them never to respond to violence with violence. He

> "If one day you find me sprawled out dead, I do not want you to retaliate with a single act of violence."[7]

also worried deeply about the safety of his wife and baby daughter. Looking at his wife and sleeping child, he thought, "They can be taken away from me at any moment."[6]

One night, the pressures were building up, and King felt he could not endure them any more. He bent over the kitchen table and prayed for strength. He felt as if a voice said to him, "Stand up for righteousness, stand up for justice, stand up for truth; and God will be at your side forever." King said of that moment, "I experienced the presence of the Divine as I had never experienced Him before."[8]

On Monday night, January 30, 1956, King's worst fears nearly came true. He was at a meeting when someone rushed up to him with frightening news. A bomb had exploded at his home with his wife and daughter inside. King rushed home to find that Coretta's foresight had kept them unhurt. Hearing a thud on the front porch, she ran with the baby toward the rear of the house to escape the blast she expected would follow. She was right: Several sticks of dynamite exploded, and the glass from the front window shattered into the room.

Thousands of outraged African Americans gathered at the bombed King home, demanding retaliation. King addressed them, saying, "We must love our white brothers

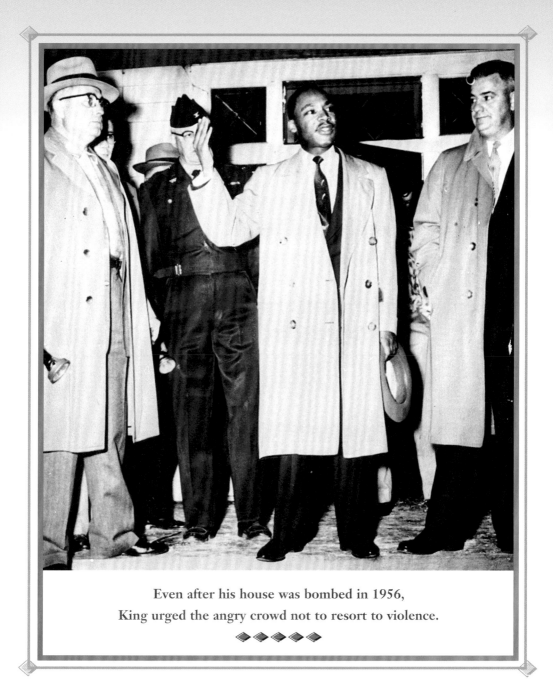

Even after his house was bombed in 1956,
King urged the angry crowd not to resort to violence.

no matter what they do to us."[9] King's powers of persuasion were so effective that violence was averted and the crowd ended up singing the hymn "Amazing Grace."

Frustrated by the economic losses to the city bus system and to downtown stores, the Montgomery County Grand Jury indicted King and 118 other civil rights leaders on charges of running an illegal boycott. King was quickly convicted and immediately filed for an appeal. The fates of the others were left suspended until King's appeal was decided. King's appeal was heard on June 4, 1956, by a three-judge panel in federal court. They held that bus segregation was unconstitutional. Not long after, the Supreme Court affirmed the decision.

King called the end of bus segregation a "glorious daybreak at the end of a long night."[10] Some angry whites responded to the decision with threats and violence, but for the most part the desegregation of the buses went smoothly. On December 20, 1956, King himself boarded a bus in Montgomery, and the white driver said cordially, "I believe you are Reverend King, aren't you?" When King said he was, the driver said, "We are glad to have you this morning."[11]

The successful Montgomery bus boycott thrust the twenty-seven-year-old King into the spotlight not only in the United States but around the world. Many news agencies from foreign countries had been observing the 381-day boycott, marveling at the thousands of adults and schoolchildren who walked to avoid riding segregated buses.

In December 1956, King and Abernathy took seats near
the front of this Montgomery bus. Next to King sat a white minister.

The next two years were filled with dramatic events in
the lives of the King family. On February 18, 1957, *Time*
magazine featured a lengthy cover story on King,
describing him as a "scholarly Negro Baptist minister who
in little more than a year has risen from nowhere to
become one of the nation's remarkable leaders of men."[12]

In March 1957, Martin and Coretta King took a trip to Africa to celebrate the country of Ghana's independence from colonial rule. It was their first long vacation since their marriage, and it was an awesome experience for the young southern couple. Fifty thousand Ghanaians, many in tribal dress, rejoiced as the British flag was lowered and the new red, green, and yellow flag of independent Ghana was raised. King commented that "both segregation in America and colonialism in Africa were based on the same thing—white supremacy and contempt for life."[13]

Later that year, King called 115 black leaders to Montgomery to discuss strategies for advancing civil rights in the United States. They formed the Southern Christian Leadership Conference (SCLC) and chose King as their president. The goal of the SCLC was to operate through black churches all over the South to support and coordinate civil rights activities. The first project was to be a drive to register as many new black voters as possible.

In October 1957, Coretta and Martin King welcomed a son, Martin Luther King, III. "Little Marty" cried so loudly that his dad said he would probably be a preacher when he grew up.[14] Also in 1957, Martin Luther King, Jr., received the NAACP's highest honor, the Spingarn Medal, in recognition of his work on behalf of African Americans.

King and other black leaders met with President Dwight D. Eisenhower in June 1958. They wanted the

The Kings held hands to say grace before they ate their meal.

president to do more for African-American civil rights. King was disappointed by what he saw as the president's conservatism, which he described as "'fixed and rigid."[15]

Back in Montgomery, Alabama, King was arrested for alleged failure to obey a police officer. His rough treatment at the hands of the police gained national attention. In the fall of 1958, he traveled north on a tour with his first book, *Stride Toward Freedom: The Montgomery Story*.

On September 19, King was signing books at Harlem's Blumstein's Department store when a black woman, Izola Curry, approached him and cried out, "Luther King, I've been after you for five years."[16] Then she lunged at King, driving a long, razor-sharp letter opener deep into his chest. King was taken to Harlem hospital, where an inter-racial team of doctors, led by Dr. Aubre D. Maynard fought to save his life. The letter-opener blade was so close to King's aorta—the body's largest artery—that if he had sneezed he would have died of a massive hemorrhage. The operation to remove the blade took three hours, and the incision in King's chest was made in the shape of a cross. Maynard commented, "He is a minister. It seemed appropriate."[17]

Izola Curry was sent to a mental hospital for the criminally insane. Speaking of her later, King said, "Get her healed."[18] Pneumonia slowed King's recovery, but he was released from the hospital on October 3, and he spent the next three weeks recuperating at a friend's house.

The following year, 1959, the Kings had an opportunity to visit India. King had looked forward to visiting the birthplace of the man whose philosophy had so shaped his thinking—Mahatma Gandhi. When he and Coretta arrived in India in February, King said he came "as a pilgrim."[19] The Kings toured the cities and rode the trains. They were touched by the poverty and the patience of so many people. King said he had found a place for America

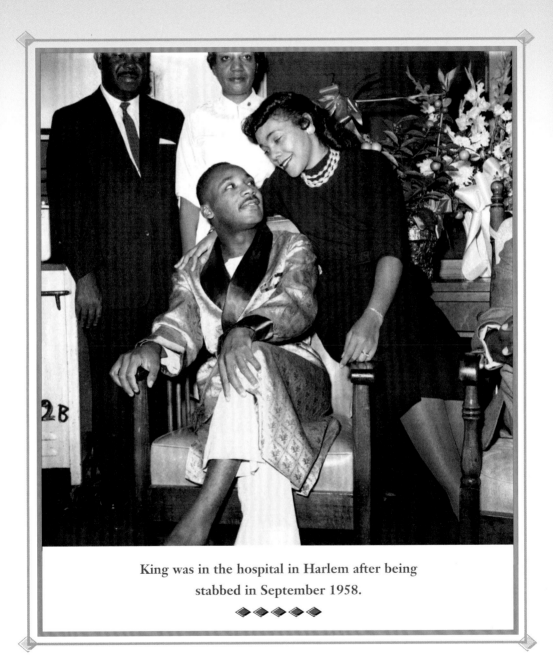

King was in the hospital in Harlem after being
stabbed in September 1958.

◆ ◆ ◆ ◆ ◆

to store all the surplus food we had—"in the wrinkled stomachs of starving people in Asia and Africa."[20] He spent a day at the spot where Gandhi started a 218-mile walk to protest injustice. King was moved by Gandhi's success in using love, goodwill, and a refusal to cooperate with evil to change his world.[21]

After India, the Kings traveled to Jerusalem, Cairo, and Athens. From his time in all these places, King felt a deeper spirituality. He resolved to sleep only four hours a night so that he could devote more time to the civil rights struggle. He also planned to set aside one day a week for fasting and meditation. With his busy schedule, he never accomplished that goal.

In November 1959, King was asked to become co-pastor of Ebenezer Baptist Church in Atlanta with his father. The SCLC was requesting more of King's time for their work, and he could not do all that and be a full-time pastor, too. King made the decision to resign from Dexter Avenue Baptist Church and return to Atlanta. In his farewell sermon to the people at Dexter, he said, "History has thrust upon me a responsibility from which I cannot turn away."[22] He and the congregation ended the service with a tearful rendition of the old hymn "Blest Be the Tie That Binds."

Within one month of Martin Luther King, Jr.'s return to Atlanta, he received word that the Montgomery Grand Jury had indicted him for tax fraud. A stunned King was crushed by this attack on his honesty and integrity.

Chapter 5

The Fight for Freedom

Martin Luther King, Jr. always prided himself on his honesty.[1] The 1960 indictment against him claimed he had falsified his Alabama state income tax returns for 1956 and 1958. Instead of the $9,150 he had reported for 1956, the government said he made $16,162. On his 1958 tax return, he had reported an income of $25,248 when it allegedly should have been $45,421. At the time, King's income as co-pastor of Ebenezer Baptist Church was $6,000 a year. The SCLC paid him $1 a year to be its president. Though royalties from books and speaking fees went into the six figures, King turned it all over to the MIA and the SCLC. He drove a 1954 Pontiac and lived in a small rented house. He had no savings to speak of, and he had no idea how he would pay back taxes and penalties—especially when he believed he did not owe them.

King even lacked the money for a decent legal defense. His friends set up an emergency legal fund to help him. Nobel Prize–winning diplomat Ralph Bunche believed that most people would know that King was innocent because, Bunche said, "It's the word of the state of Alabama against the word of Martin Luther King. There is no question in my mind which the country will accept."[2] King himself had no such confidence. He lamented that "many people will think I am guilty." He was sure he would be convicted when he went to trial and, he said, "people will believe that I took money that didn't belong to me."[3]

King fell into a deep depression. His enemies had tried fire bombing his house, arresting him on false charges, and harassing him with death threats. Now they were cutting to the heart of King's character. He feared that the charges would destroy his effectiveness in the civil rights struggle. For a while he did not want to face anybody, and he canceled some speeches. But then he decided he had to stand up to this false accusation and get on with his work.

King traveled to Montgomery, Alabama, to join hands with college students who were protesting segregated lunch counters. It was his message to the outside world that he would not be intimidated, even by the income tax evasion accusation.

In May 1960, King met with his legal team. They had already spent $10,000 preparing his defense. King was very upset, saying it was "immoral and impractical" to waste so much money on a defense that was bound to fail.[4] Though certain of his conviction in the Alabama courts, King pinned his hopes on an appeal to the federal courts. His lawyers, on the other hand, kept assuring him that the case against him was so ridiculous that not even a white jury in Alabama would believe it.

On Monday, May 23, 1960, King stood trial. His attorneys argued that the whole case was a frame-up. When the prosecution presented its case, the star witness admitted that King was an honest man. Still, King looked at those twelve white men sitting in the jury box, and he thought he knew what was coming—a conviction. The jury deliberated, and on Saturday they gave their verdict: not guilty. King was astonished. He said he had learned a great lesson: "What started out as a bigoted, prejudiced jury" had chosen "the path of justice."[5] With the tax case out of the way, King returned his attention to the sit-ins at segregated lunch counters in the South.

In Atlanta, King met with seventy-five students who were sitting in at the lunch counter at Rich's Department Store. Dick Rich, the owner, cried when he saw King with the demonstrators because he knew the pressure and publicity would mount quickly. King and the students were arrested, and King refused to pay the $500 bond that would release him from jail until his case came before the judge. He insisted he would stay in jail "ten years if necessary."[6]

Dr. King showed his support for protestors outside Rich's Department Store in Atlanta.

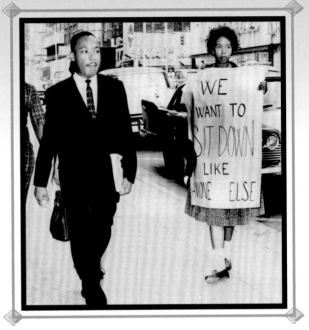

◆ ◆ ◆ ◆ ◆

Officials in Atlanta, not wanting the bad publicity, dropped all charges against King. But the harassment did not end there. The traffic court judge from neighboring De Kalb County ordered that King be held on another charge. Earlier, King had been cited for driving without a valid license. His Alabama license had expired and he did not yet have a Georgia license. For that offense he had been charged $25 and placed on probation for a year. If he were arrested again during the year for any offense, he would be subject to prison. The arrest at Rich's Department Store was deemed a violation of King's probation.

King was sentenced to four months at hard labor for the probation violation. His supporters were shocked by this turn of events. For King to be ordered to tough Reidsville Prison for violating probation on a minor traffic offense was unheard of. Coretta King, five months

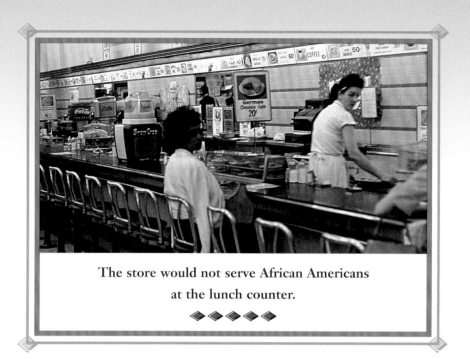

**The store would not serve African Americans
at the lunch counter.**

pregnant with their third child, wept in the courtroom. It was the first time she ever cried in public during all the civil rights struggles. When his wife visited him in jail before he was transferred to Reidsville, King told her to "be strong" for him.[7]

In the middle of that night, several men came to King's cell shouting for him to get up. A flashlight beam was thrown in his face. King knew all too well that black prisoners roused from jail at night sometimes disappeared. He was not sure what was happening as handcuffs were snapped on his wrists and chains clamped to his legs. The handcuffs were so tight that they bit into his flesh as he was hauled out to a sheriff's car.

After a three-hundred-mile drive, King saw the sign for

Reidsville Prison looming in the darkness. He was hustled inside and given a prison uniform, white with green stripes down the pant legs. He was placed in the kind of cell reserved for hardened criminals. Cockroaches darted across the cell walls. It was bitter cold. The next day, the guards brought lunch, black-eyed peas and greens, which tasted so bad King could not eat it. He fell ill with a cold and lay feverish on his bunk, wondering what was happening.

Unknown to King, events on the outside were moving swiftly. Massachusetts senator John F. Kennedy, the Democratic candidate for president in the 1960 election, heard of King's plight and called Coretta King to express his concern. Then he called the judge who had sentenced King and demanded to know why bail had not been granted in this case. The judge changed his ruling, and King was immediately released on bail. Word of Kennedy's intervention swept through the black community.

The presidential election was held two weeks later, and Kennedy won with 75 percent of black voters. It was a close election, and their votes made a difference.

On January 30, 1961, the Kings' third child, Dexter Scott, was born. Dr. King had high hopes for the newly inaugurated John F. Kennedy. He saw in the young president a real chance to have the federal government energetically on the side of the civil rights struggle. But after meeting with Kennedy and his brother, Attorney General Robert Kennedy, King was dissatisfied. The

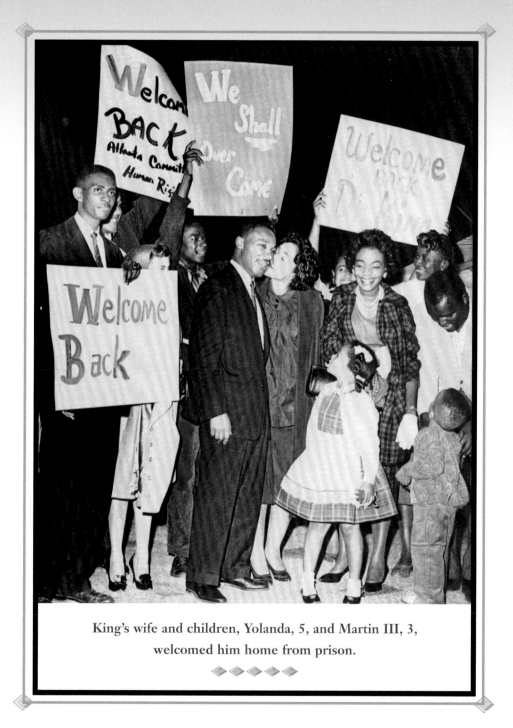

King's wife and children, Yolanda, 5, and Martin III, 3, welcomed him home from prison.

meetings were cordial, but King did not feel that President Kennedy saw ending segregation as a major priority in his administration. Still, as time went by, King hoped the president would become an important ally for civil rights.

In the spring of 1961, the Congress of Racial Equality (CORE), a civil rights group trying to end segregation, sent a large number of young people, called freedom riders, to challenge the segregation laws in interstate travel. The Freedom Riders, who were black and white, left Washington aboard Greyhound buses. When they reached Alabama, they were attacked by mobs wielding sticks, brass knuckles, and lead pipes. In one instance, a mob surrounded a bus filled with freedom riders and set it on fire. King saw television coverage of the violent events and flew at once to Montgomery.

At a mass rally at Reverend Ralph Abernathy's church, King spoke while ten thousand angry white people milled outside, shouting and threatening to storm the building. King called Robert Kennedy, who called Alabama governor John Malcolm Patterson and asked for protection for the blacks in the church. Patterson declared martial law: The government would call in the military to keep order. National Guardsmen moved to disperse the white mob. As a result of this and other demonstrations, the Interstate Commerce Commission outlawed segregation on all forms of public transportation.

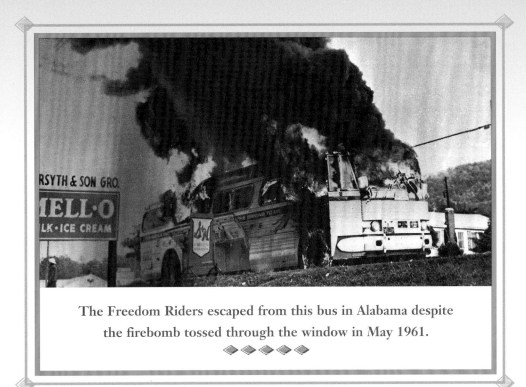

The Freedom Riders escaped from this bus in Alabama despite
the firebomb tossed through the window in May 1961.

◆ ◆ ◆ ◆ ◆

In Albany, Georgia, the Student Nonviolent
Coordinating Committee (SNCC, pronounced "snick")
was mounting a protest against segregation on buses and
trains. In spite of the federal government's desegregation
orders, buses and trains continued to be segregated.
SNCC held a freedom march in Albany, and five hundred
young people were jailed. Many could not afford bail, so
they remained behind bars.

Dr. William Anderson, a black physician, called on
Martin Luther King, Jr., to come down to help what was
now called the Albany Movement. King came on
December 15, 1961, with the intention of making a speech

to energize the movement, but he stayed to join in the march. On December 16, King and many others were arrested, charged with parading without a permit. King vowed to spend Christmas in jail to illustrate his commitment to the movement. But city officials bailed him out to prevent the story from making major national news.

When King arrived in Albany, he thought the African-American leadership was united, as it had been in Montgomery during the successful bus boycott. Unfortunately it was seriously divided. SNCC was in charge, and the NAACP was not supportive. There was rivalry and jealousy among black leaders.

The local black people of Albany loved King, but the leadership was suspicious of him. One black leader said the Albany Movement needed no "outside help," rejecting King's aid.[8] Though the Albany Movement was an ambitious effort to attack segregation on many fronts, the disunity caused it to fail.

King returned to Atlanta and began work on his second book, *Strength to Love*, in early 1963. During the previous seven years, King had spent more than 75 percent of his time away from home, taking part in civil rights struggles throughout the South. He tried to make the most of what little time he had with his family.

"We had quality time," daughter Yoki later recalled. "Whenever he was home it was as if we were the whole world."[9] King enjoyed lifting the children to the top of the

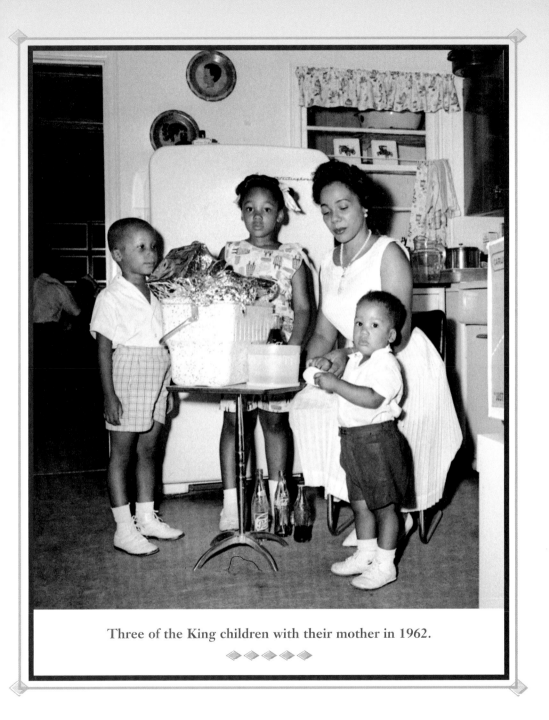

Three of the King children with their mother in 1962.

refrigerator and then having them jump into his arms. As the children grew older, they would jump to him from the stairway banister. He never missed a catch.

When Yoki wanted to go to Funtown, a segregated amusement park that had just opened in Atlanta, the Kings had to explain to her that it was not possible because of her skin color, but they assured her that one day this would change. On March 28, 1963, the Kings' fourth child, Bernice Albertine, was born.

A few days later, King turned his attention to Birmingham, Alabama. He had two goals for Birmingham: The first was to force white leaders to begin desegregation. African Americans would apply pressure by boycotting downtown department stores. King's second goal was to draw federal attention to injustices against black people. He planned to use large protest demonstrations to get this message across.

Black leaders were united in Birmingham, but they faced a brutal opponent in the person of Theophilus Eugene "Bull" Connor, Commissioner of Public Safety and supervisor of the police and fire departments. Connor was known for his extreme racism and for using harsh tactics to crush opposition. King anticipated drawing nationwide attention to Birmingham when Connor's troops confronted the demonstrators. King counted on Connor's bullying tactics to rouse mass public sympathy for the cause of civil rights.

Chapter 6

Birmingham

King called Birmingham, Alabama, "the most thoroughly segregated city in the country."[1] On Good Friday, April 12, 1963, King began his nonviolent attack on that segregation. Clad in denim jeans and a rough work shirt, showing his readiness to be arrested, King led a march in downtown Birmingham. After walking five blocks, the group was confronted by Commissioner Bull Connor, who told them all they were under arrest for an illegal demonstration. When they arrived at the Birmingham jail, all the protesters except King were put into a large cell. King was sent to a small, dark cell by himself. King later called those early hours of imprisonment "the longest, most frustrating and bewildering hours I have lived."[2] There was no bed in the cell. Only a set of bare steel springs was provided. No blankets or pillows were furnished.

When President Kennedy learned of the harsh conditions under which King was being held, he contacted the authorities in Birmingham and warned them that an inquiry was under way. Immediately, conditions for King improved. He received a mattress to sleep on, a blanket, and permission to shower and shave. Kennedy called Coretta King to assure her that "we've checked on your husband, and he's all right."[3] King's jailers then permitted him to take a call from his wife.

King had no writing paper in his cell, but he wanted to record his impressions. At first he used margins of the *Birmingham News* and scraps of toilet paper to write on. A black guard then passed him some scraps of paper, and finally his lawyer gave him a notepad. King's writings from his jail cell became "Letter from Birmingham Jail," a powerful statement telling black people that they should not wait any longer for their rights. King wrote, "This 'Wait' has always meant 'Never.' We have waited for more than 340 years for our constitutional and God-given rights."[4] King's nine-thousand-word letter has become a classic in protest literature.

On April 20, King and the others arrested paid their bail and were released. On April 23, King was convicted, then released on bail again while he filed an appeal.

Another big demonstration was planned, consisting largely of black children and teenagers. On May 2, a protest that would be known as the Children's Crusade got under way with 959 youngsters ranging in age from six to sixteen. A police officer confronted an eight-year-old

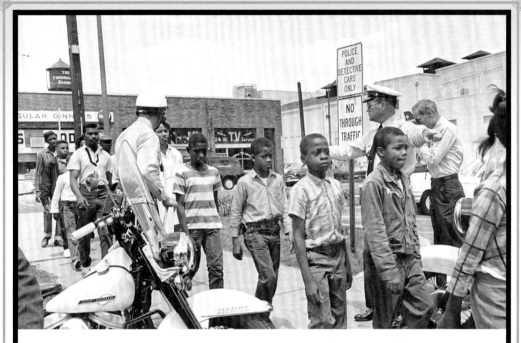

Birmingham police arrested these black schoolchildren
for their peaceful protest near the city hall, May 4, 1963.

and demanded to know what she wanted. "Freedom!" the little girl shouted.[5] All the young people were arrested. There was not enough room for them in the local jails, so they were held in outdoor pens in the hot sun without sanitary facilities. The Birmingham authorities hoped the unpleasant experience would discourage the children from further protests.

Another demonstration quickly followed. The group, which included children and adults, began shouting, "We want freedom." A frustrated Bull Connor ordered his firemen to "Let 'em have it."[6] After one-hundred-pound German shepherds charged into the crowd, biting some of the marchers, high-pressure hoses were aimed at the protestors. The stream of water was so powerful that people were smashed against buildings and bark was stripped from trees. As children were swept down the street, some suffered broken arms and ribs. Connor's men then waded into the crowd, beating the protesters with fists, feet, and billy clubs.

President Kennedy watched the violence on television. He said the sight of children being attacked like that made him "sick."[7] Kennedy added that he could well understand the unwillingness of blacks to wait any longer for equality.

The outrage across the country was so great that Birmingham city officials finally agreed to negotiate with the African-American community. King and his allies made four demands. First, complete desegregation of all facilities in the downtown stores; second, the hiring of blacks in sales and clerical positions; third, the institution of a permanent biracial committee to work on desegregating the whole city. The fourth and final demand was the release from jail of all the protestors.

When Birmingham officials agreed to the demands, King was overjoyed. But the results of the agreement were not all positive. Angry whites resented the advances blacks had made. Some resorted to violence. The front of

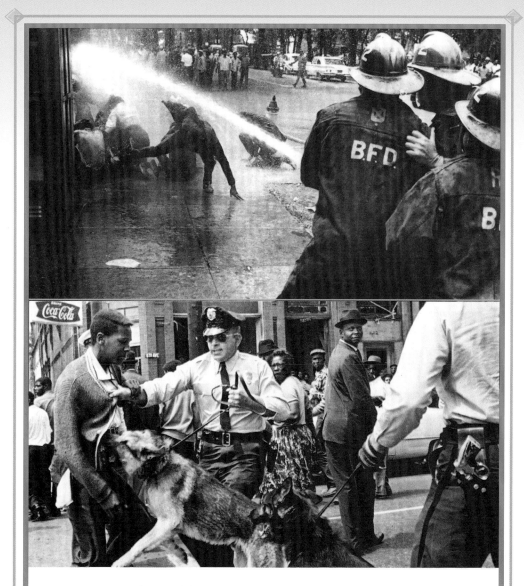

Birmingham, Alabama, May 1963: *Top*, Firemen blast their
high-pressure hoses to break up a crowd of protesters. *Bottom*, Police
set their attack dogs against this seventeen-year-old boy.

A.D. King's home was blown away by a bomb. Still, the struggle in Birmingham had been a success, and it firmly established Martin Luther King, Jr., as the national leader in the drive for black equality. It also raised the prestige of the SCLC as an organization that could be depended upon to produce results.

King had been thrust into national prominence by the Birmingham success, and he was greatly in demand all over the country for speeches. He spoke to ten thousand people in Chicago. He addressed twenty-five thousand in Los Angeles, and a hundred and twenty-five thousand in Detroit. With the momentum so strong in favor of black equality, Attorney General Robert Kennedy urged his brother to initiate major civil rights legislation. In June 1963 President Kennedy introduced sweeping legislation to outlaw segregation in interstate public accommodations throughout the country. The federal government would be authorized to force school integration and shut off aid to all programs that practiced discrimination.

The news caused joy in the civil rights movement and bitter resentment among white segregationists who did not want anything to change. The day after Kennedy's announcement, Medgar Evers, an activist in the Mississippi NAACP, was shot to death in front of his house in Jackson, Mississippi. The state of Mississippi disregarded all integration efforts by the federal government, and civil rights marchers there were brutally beaten. On

◆◆◆◆◆◆◆◆◆◆◆◆◆◆◆◆◆◆◆◆◆◆◆◆◆◆◆

Medgar Evers

Medgar Evers, Mississippi's best-known activist for civil rights, became a martyr to the struggle for equality. As field secretary of the NAACP in Mississippi, Evers motivated African Americans to register to vote, organized a boycott of stores in Jackson, Mississippi, and worked to end segregation. The enemies of civil rights hated Evers, and murdered him. This first assassination of a black civil rights leader set off race riots as far away as Harlem, New York. Martin Luther King, Jr., came to Evers's funeral and, as he always did, counseled nonviolence even in the face of murder.

June 22, 1963, President Kennedy invited King and other civil rights leaders to the White House to address the problem.

A. Philip Randolph, who in 1925 had founded the largest black labor group in America, the Brotherhood of Sleeping Car Porters, came up with an idea at the meeting. He urged a large march on Washington, D.C., made up of blacks and sympathetic whites, calling for immediate racial equality in America. President Kennedy did not like the idea, but King embraced it. Kennedy pleaded with King to abandon the plan, warning him that it might lead to bloodshed and a backlash against black people.[8]

"Mr. President," King insisted, "the masses are restless,

and we will march. We will have a march on Washington."[9] Kennedy continued to argue that the march would soon be out of control, ending in violence. He feared his civil rights legislation would be doomed. But King and the other black leaders would not be moved. They began to make plans for a summer march on Washington.

At this time, Martin Luther King, Jr., was under investigation by J. Edgar Hoover of the Federal Bureau of Investigation (FBI). For many years, Hoover had been convinced that the Communist Party in the United States was using the civil rights movement to recruit members and undermine the U.S. government.

Ever since Russia had adopted a Communist government in 1917, many people had feared that Communism would take over the United States. After World War II, Communism had spread to several countries, with Eastern Europe, China, and Cuba becoming Communist. Communist leaders hoped to spread their ideology worldwide, often by infiltrating groups and then starting a revolution.

Under Communism there is no personal property. Everything is owned by the government, and all property is to be shared equally among the citizens. There is also no freedom of speech, religion, right to assemble, or any of the other rights Americans take for granted.

Officials like Hoover worried about the influence of Communism in the United States. So the FBI kept an

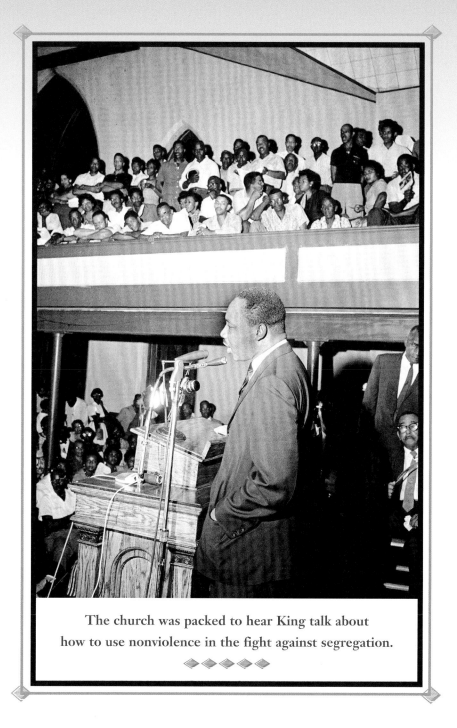

The church was packed to hear King talk about
how to use nonviolence in the fight against segregation.

"enemies list" of people seen as threats to the American way of life.

Martin Luther King, Jr., was on the list of America's most dangerous enemies. Although King was on record as denouncing Communism as an atheistic fraud, Hoover ignored this fact. Hoover was determined to gather evidence against King that would prove him to be a Communist agent. He asked Attorney General Robert Kennedy for permission to plant listening devices in King's offices and in hotels and motels where King stayed. Kennedy granted this request.

Unaware of the massive effort to discredit him as a Communist agent, King issued a call for all blacks and whites friendly to the cause to make plans to come to Washington by car, train, bus, or plane. The march was scheduled for August 28, 1963, and the theme was "jobs and freedom."

Hoover hoped he could amass enough evidence against King before the march to destroy his credibility. He feared that a successful march would catapult King into such a powerful position that he could no longer be stopped.

Kaneland Middle School
1N...
Maple Park, IL ...01

Chapter 7

"I Have a Dream"

On the morning of August 28, 1963, almost one hundred thousand blacks and whites were gathering around the Lincoln Memorial in Washington, D.C. Another one hundred and fifty thousand were pouring into the city from highways, airports, and bus terminals. By the time Martin Luther King, Jr., faced the audience to make his speech, there were about two hundred thousand blacks and sixty thousand whites assembled in the great mall between the Lincoln Memorial and the Capitol Rotunda.

Here, King delivered the most famous speech of his life, known as "I Have a Dream." It was a passionate, eloquent call for equality of all people. "I have a dream," King said in one of the most memorable lines, "that my four little children will one day live in a nation where they will not be judged by the color of their skin, but by the content of their character."[1] King concluded his speech with the hope that "*all* God's children, black men and white men, Jews and gentiles, Protestants and Catholics, will be able to join hands and sing in the words of that old Negro spiritual, 'Free at last! Free at last! Thank God Almighty, we are free at last!'"[2]

The stunning speech, delivered with great power and emotion, left the crowd shouting with joy. Many were weeping and crying out King's name. President Kennedy, who had worried so much about the march, was delighted by how smoothly everything went. He invited King and some of the other march organizers to the White House for lunch. It was a moment of triumph for King and the whole civil rights movement. All the other demonstrations had been leading to this day, and now it appeared that the nation was uniting in a desire to make the dream of equality a reality for all Americans.

J. Edgar Hoover was unhappy at the attention King was getting. He had described King as "the most dangerous Negro of the future in this nation from the standpoint of Communism."[3] Now it seemed to Hoover that this dangerous man was making even more serious inroads to the heart of the nation. Hoover's agents had not stopped King before the march, but they did not give up.

After the march, King and other civil rights leaders went to their suite in the Willard Hotel in Washington. Inside, everyone was in high spirits after the success of the day.

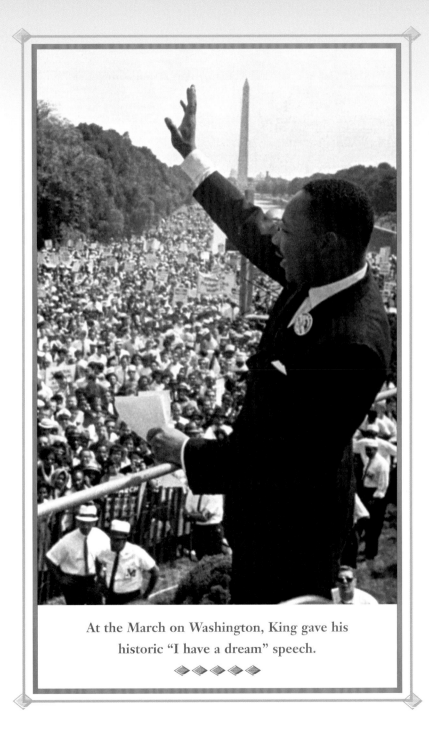

At the March on Washington, King gave his
historic "I have a dream" speech.

The FBI knew King and his party would celebrate there after the march, and the agents were ready. They had planted listening devices in the suite and were recording everything. After the party, the tapes were retrieved and sent to Hoover. He listened to them, then sent them on to Attorney General Kennedy. Robert Kennedy agreed to increase the spying on King, and electronic devices were planted in King's Atlanta home phone and in all SCLC telephones to check for Communist connections.

Attorney General Kennedy thought that if the tapes revealed no Communist connections to King, then Hoover would give up his campaign against King. However, if any proof were uncovered, Kennedy planned to confront King with the evidence and demand that he cut off all contact with friends who were members of the Communist Party.

Meanwhile, Hoover was busy making copies of the Willard Hotel tapes, hoping these would undermine King. He sent copies to the White House, the secretary of state, the Defense Department, the CIA, and the Joint Chiefs of Staff. At the time, King had no idea that all this was happening.

On Sunday morning, September 15, 1963, one of the most horrendous acts of violence committed during the civil rights struggle took place. A bomb exploded in Birmingham's Sixteenth Street Baptist Church, a center for rallies and marches. Four young girls in the back of the church were putting on their choir robes, all four died instantly. King was shocked and horrified by the "sin and evil" of this act.[4] He came as close to bitter despair as he ever would in his life. King was preaching at Ebenezer Baptist Church when the bombing took place, and he traveled immediately to Birmingham. At

> "If men were this bestial was there any hope? Was there any way out?"[6]

the funeral for the girls, King described them as "heroines of a holy crusade for freedom and human dignity."[5]

The year 1963 was a time of triumph and challenge for King. His schedule became busier than ever. Between fund-raising, lobbying, writing, making 350 speeches, and traveling more than 275,000 miles, he was away from home most of the time. He had started his third book, *Why We Can't Wait*, about the Birmingham campaign. Desegregation was becoming a reality throughout the South, but the pace was uneven. In Atlanta, the city council ended all segregation, and that included Funtown. Finally Yoki King could enjoy the spinning rides and cotton candy at the amusement park. While King and his daughter were there, white strangers approached them with friendly smiles and warm greetings.

King's personal life in 1963 was, by his own admission, "troubled."[7] King, who had been raised in comfort, sometimes felt guilty that he had not suffered as most of his black brothers and sisters had. He worried that he had not

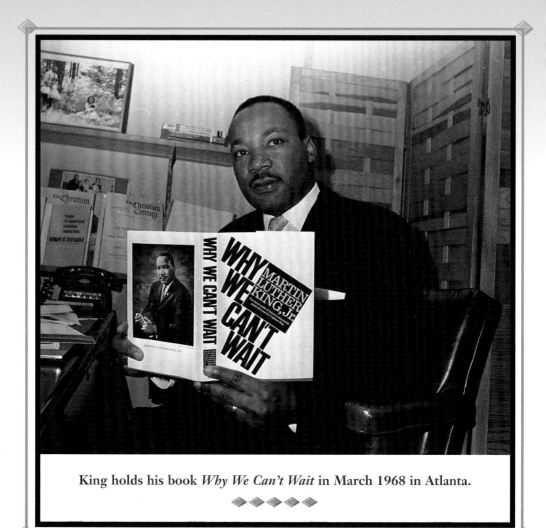

King holds his book *Why We Can't Wait* in March 1968 in Atlanta.

earned all the praise he received.[8] King kept looking for ways to sacrifice himself for the cause in the hopes of being more deserving as a leader. He had a very strong conscience, and he lamented the times when he had fallen short of his high ideals.[9] "I am conscious of two Martin Luther Kings," he said later, describing a constant battle against his "lower self."[10] His feelings of guilt and self-doubt brought on bouts of insomnia and stomach pains. King's stomach problems were not helped by his huge appetite. He enjoyed sampling food from everybody else's plate in addition to finishing off his own meal.

On November 22, 1963, King was working on his book and half listening to the radio. When he heard the shocking news that President John F. Kennedy had been assassinated, he said to his wife, "This is sick. You just can't do right and survive in this nation."[11] Deeply shaken and close to tears, King said, "This is going to happen to me too. I just realized it. It's true, Corrie. I'll never see my fortieth birthday."[12] Coretta King had no words of solace for her husband.[13]

King attended the funeral of President Kennedy at St. Matthew's Cathedral in Washington, D.C. The new president, Lyndon Johnson, vowed that in honor of the slain Kennedy, he would see that the civil rights bill was passed. King met with Johnson in December 1963. Although he respected the new president, he did not have the same relationship with him that he had had with Kennedy.

On January 3, 1964, *Time* magazine named King "Man of the Year." He was the first African American to receive that recognition and only the second black person. (The first was Ethiopian leader Haile Selassie.)

King now turned to the civil rights struggle going on in St. Augustine, Florida. During a protest march against a segregated hotel, he and his fellow marchers were arrested. King was roughly treated and shoved into a jail cell. He said of the experience, "I've been in fifteen jails, but this is the first time that I have been treated like a hog."[14] The St. Augustine campaign achieved only modest gains, but in Washington, the legislation known as the 1964 Civil Rights Act was passed and signed by President Johnson.

King came to see President Johnson sign the Civil Rights Act of 1964.

The bill banned discrimination in jobs, voting, and all public accommodations.

As King well knew, passing a new Civil Rights Act would not change people's hearts. Desegregation would not come easily to the Deep South. In June 1964, three young civil rights workers came to Mississippi to register black voters. Andrew Goodman and Michael Schwerner were white. James Chaney was black. The three men were arrested—supposedly for a traffic violation—in Neshoba County, Mississippi. They were released and told to get out of the area. Some members of the Ku Klux Klan followed the trio, overtook their car, and drove them out to a lonely road.

> "We must combine the toughness of the serpent and the softness of the dove—a tough mind and a tender heart."[15]

When it was discovered that the three men were missing, it was immediately feared that they had met with foul play. A Klansman eventually told the FBI where to search, and their bodies were discovered. They had been beaten, shot, and buried under an earthen dam in the hopes that their graves might be overlooked. Saddened by the new atrocity, and exhausted from his heavy work schedule, Martin Luther King, Jr., checked into a hospital. Coretta visited her husband there with some great news—he had been awarded the Nobel Peace Prize for 1964.

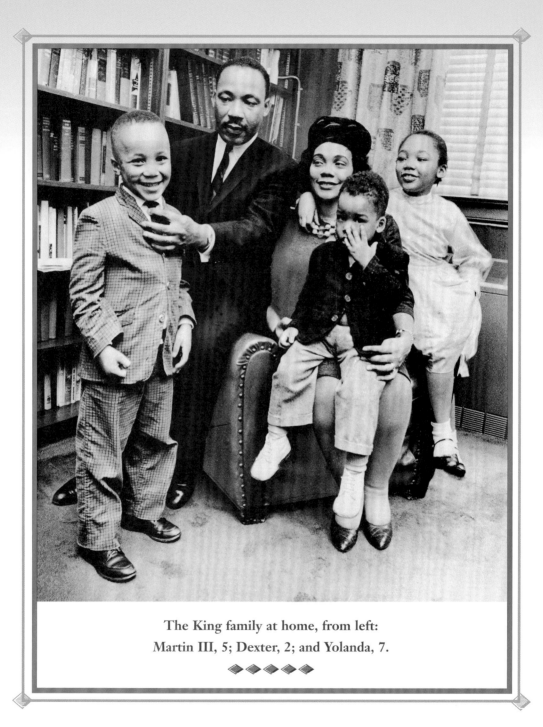

The King family at home, from left:
Martin III, 5; Dexter, 2; and Yolanda, 7.

Nobel Prize and Vietnam

Martin Luther King, Jr., said the Nobel Peace Prize was not a personal honor but a tribute to the "discipline, wise restraint, and majestic courage of millions of gallant Negro and white persons of good will who have followed a nonviolent course."[1] He pledged to donate the entire $54,000 prize to the cause of civil rights.

Still recovering from exhaustion at St. Joseph's Hospital in Atlanta, King received a visit from the city's Catholic Archbishop Paul Halliman. The Archbishop congratulated King on receiving the Nobel Prize, and blessed him. Then, to King's surprise, Halliman dropped to his knees and asked King, "May I receive your blessing?" Humbled by the gesture, King obliged.[2]

King went to Oslo, Norway, to receive the Nobel Peace Prize in a moving ceremony. But his elation was not

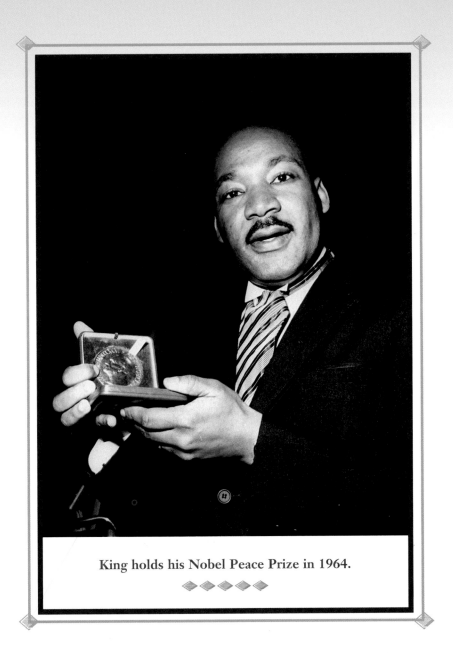

King holds his Nobel Peace Prize in 1964.

Alfred Nobel

Alfred Nobel was a wealthy inventor who lived in Sweden in the 1800s. He invented dynamite in 1867. Then he invented an even more powerful explosive called blasting gelatin. These explosives were useful in mining, road building, tunnel blasting, and war. To offset the false impression that he cared only about war, Nobel established a fund to award the most important work in physics, chemistry, physiology or medicine, and peace. Every year someone in the world is awarded the Nobel Peace Prize based on his or her contribution to peace and the good of humanity. Among the Americans so honored have been Presidents Theodore Roosevelt, Woodrow Wilson, and Jimmy Carter. United Nations mediator Ralph Bunche received a Nobel Peace Prize, as did Mother Teresa of Calcutta, India.

to last. J. Edgar Hoover, who had described King as "the most notorious liar in America," believed that he now had the evidence to discredit King.[3] In January 1965, Coretta Scott King found an anonymous package mailed to her from Miami, Florida. Inside the package was a tape and a note addressed to King, which said in part, "King, like all frauds your end is approaching." Along with crude insults, the note also suggested that King had "but one way out," hinting that he should commit suicide.[4]

Coretta King called her husband, and they both read the note. It claimed the tape was a copy of the FBI recording of the party in the Willard Hotel.

The FBI expected King to be embarrassed that his partying had been caught on tape. King insisted that the tape be played with Coretta and some civil rights allies present. Years later, commenting on the contents of the tape, Coretta King said, "We found much of it unintelligible. We concluded that there was nothing in the tape to discredit him."[5] However, the whole incident left King shaken and frightened. "They are out to break me," he said. "They are out to get me, harass me, break my spirit." A despondent King, unafraid to admit to his own shortcomings, insisted that whatever happened in his life was "between me and my God."[6]

For a while King deliberated whether or not he should keep the commitments he had made to speak. After some soul searching, he decided to go on as usual. King said that he believed God would not judge him for his mistakes, but for "the total bent" of his life.[7]

Undaunted by the failure of the tape to ruin King, the FBI continued to watch him. Everywhere King went, there was electronic surveillance. His hotel and meeting rooms were all bugged. There was a massive effort to find something to bring him down. The bugging became a joke to King and his allies. Before every meeting, they

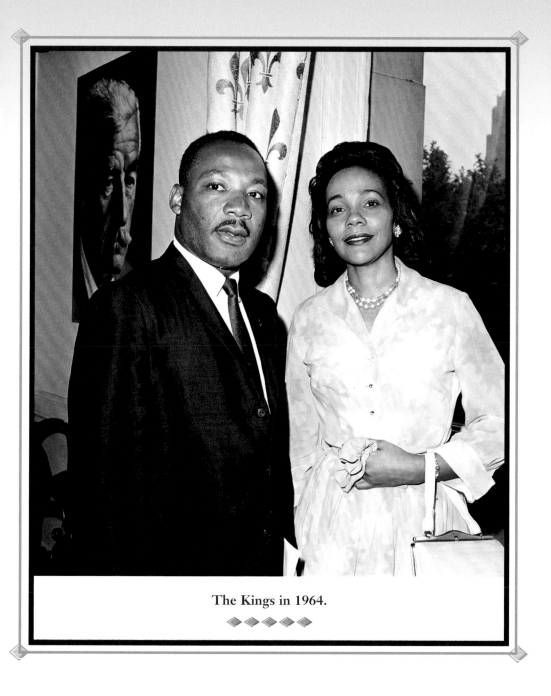

The Kings in 1964.

would acknowledge the spying by greeting J. Edgar Hoover as if he were in the room: "How are you doing?"[8]

A march for voting rights was scheduled to begin March 7, 1965, in Selma, Alabama, and end in Montgomery. King was not planning to be a part of the march, but he watched developments closely. Six hundred and fifty people headed for the Edmund Pettus Bridge on their way to Montgomery, and there they were confronted by Alabama state troopers. When the marchers would not obey orders to turn around and return to Selma, the troopers on horseback charged into the crowd. They rode right over the marchers, knocking them down and beating them with clubs. The troopers, in gas masks, then released a stream of gas that left the marchers sick and gasping.

All over America that night, television programming was interrupted to show the brutal violence. President Johnson looked at the gruesome photos of wounded marchers and denounced what had happened. King, guilt-ridden that he was not there with the beleaguered marchers, rushed to Alabama. On March 9, 1965, King helped lead another march toward Montgomery. The more than three thousand marchers were halted, but this time there was no violence.

President Johnson addressed a joint session of Congress on March 15, 1965, calling what had happened to the marchers "an American tragedy." He asked for swift

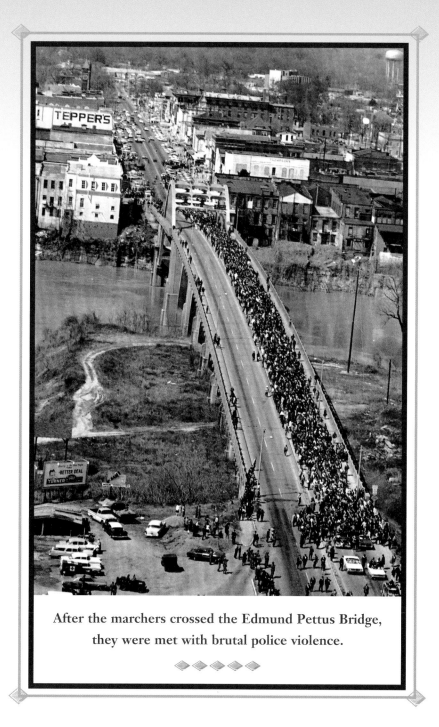

After the marchers crossed the Edmund Pettus Bridge,
they were met with brutal police violence.

passage of the 1965 Civil Rights Act, which would eliminate all qualifying tests for voter registration.[9]

On August 5, 1965, the Civil Rights Act was signed by the president. King was grateful for President Johnson's efforts to advance civil rights. However another issue was about to drive a serious wedge between the two men.

At the end of 1965, almost 185,000 American soldiers were fighting in a war in Vietnam. Casualties mounted as the United States tried to keep South Vietnam from becoming a Communist nation like North Vietnam. Many Americans opposed the war, but President Johnson insisted that unless the Communists were stopped in Vietnam, all Asia was in danger of falling to Communism.

Martin Luther King, Jr., believed the war was sapping the moral and economic energy of the United States. Americans were bombing Vietnam and enemy camps in surrounding countries, and there were many civilian casualties. After seeing magazine photos of severely burned Vietnamese children, King vowed to "do everything I can to end that war."[10] But he did not speak publicly against the war at that time. Instead, he turned his attention to poverty and racial injustice in Chicago.

After many years of fighting discrimination in the South, King now concerned himself with the plight of poor people in the slums of Chicago, whose lives were scarred by unemployment and poor housing. It was King's first campaign in the North.

To show his commitment, King moved his family into a run-down apartment in the tenement district of Chicago at the intersection of Sixteenth Street and Hamlin Avenue. When Coretta King first saw this grim part of the city, she lamented, "There's nothing green in sight."[11] It would be the first time King had ever lived like this. The house had two bedrooms, a kitchen, and bathroom. The gas stove did not work, and plaster was crumbling and falling.

King decided to focus on housing segregation, leading marchers into white neighborhoods in a nonviolent demand for change. Later, historians would generally conclude that King's Chicago Freedom Movement of 1966 was a failure that did not bring about reforms.

As the Vietnam War raged on, Martin Luther King, Jr., made his first public antiwar speech on April 4, 1967.

Black Power

When Martin Luther King, Jr., went to Chicago to fight for decent housing for the poor, he met angry young blacks who belonged to a rising new segment of the African-American community. This militant group called for "Black Power," and some of its members rejected King's commitment to nonviolence. Groups like the Black Liberation Army, the Black Students Union, and the Black Panthers showed disdain for King's methods. They promoted ghetto riots and even armed rebellion.

In April 1967, Dr. King spoke passionately against what he called America's "tragic, reckless adventure in Vietnam."

He called for an end to the bombing and for immediate peace negotiations. "Somehow this madness must cease," he said. "We must stop now. I speak as a child of God and brother to the suffering poor of Vietnam."[12]

A firestorm of criticism followed. Respected magazines like *Newsweek* and *Life*, and newspapers including *The New York Times* and the *Washington Post*, all denounced King's remarks. Many of King's loyal friends—such as Whitney Young of the National Urban League, Roy Wilkins of the NAACP, sports icon Jackie Robinson, and African-American senator Edward Brooke—condemned King's position on the war. Even the SCLC asked King to be silent on the subject.

King's friend Andrew Young described the civil rights leader as being "almost reduced to tears," but "on fire with determination."[13] "I know I'm right," King told his wife. "I know this is an unjust and evil war."[14]

King refused to retreat from his position and his public comments, admitting that it was "a low period in my life."[15] He insisted that the Vietnam War "practically destroyed Vietnam and left thousands of American and Vietnamese youth maimed and mutilated," adding that "we [must] end the nightmarish war and free our souls."[16] King called for an end to the war.

In December 1967, Martin Luther King was planning an even larger campaign on behalf of poor people of all colors. He wanted to bring thousands of poor Americans to the Washington Monument, where they would put up a tent city to symbolize the lack of decent housing for the poor. President Johnson opposed the idea, and more criticism came King's way.

After a brief vacation in Jamaica and Mexico, the Kings returned to the United States to learn of a labor crisis in Memphis, Tennessee. Black sanitation workers needed his help. This would turn out to be King's last battle.

Chapter 9

"Free at Last"

Seeking escape from a driving rainstorm in Memphis, on February 1, 1968, two black sanitation workers crawled into the rear of a garbage truck. When somebody accidentally threw a switch, they were crushed to death. Their families were left penniless, and because sanitation workers received no benefits, their families' situation was desperate. When the families appealed to the city for help, they were turned down.

On that same rainy day, black sewer workers were sent home without pay, but their white supervisors were kept on, with pay. These incidents triggered the Memphis sanitation workers to strike. The sanitation and sewer workers of Memphis received no medical insurance, no worker's compensation to provide a temporary salary in case they were injured on the job, and no overtime pay when they worked more than eight hours a day. They were the lowest-paid workers in the city. To improve their conditions, they formed a union to represent them in negotiations with Memphis authorities. The city refused to recognize the union.

The Memphis workers walked off the job and went on strike, carrying signs proclaiming "I Am a Man."[1] The city threatened to fire them all and bring in new workers to replace them. A local judge issued an injunction ordering all protest marchers to stop. The workers of Memphis

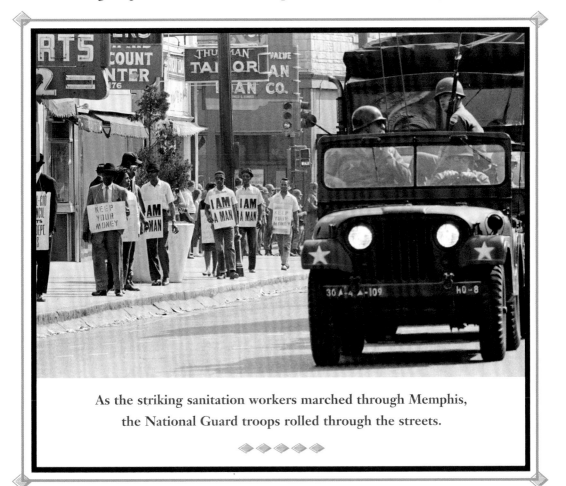

As the striking sanitation workers marched through Memphis, the National Guard troops rolled through the streets.

were losing hope, and they did not know where to turn. Reverend James Lawson of Memphis, an old friend of Martin Luther King's, asked King to come to Memphis and lend his prestige and support to the cause.

The SCLC staff tried to discourage King from going to Memphis. He had a heavy schedule of speeches in Georgia, Alabama, and Mississippi. The Poor People's Campaign was getting started, and the march on Washington to build a tent city there would be a huge undertaking. King's aides insisted that he did not have time to go to Memphis. King responded, "These are poor folks. If we don't stop for them, then we don't need to go to Washington. These are part of the people we're going there for."[2]

To make time for the people in Memphis, King quickly crisscrossed the South, speaking to thousands of people. In just one day, he stopped in seven towns in Mississippi, making speeches in all of them. His energy was unbounded. Once he had fulfilled all his speaking engagements, he was free to help his friends in Memphis.

On March 18, King arrived in Memphis. He conferred with local leaders and then went to the Masonic Temple to make a speech. He expected to just give a short pep talk, but when he arrived, fifteen thousand people awaited him.

King's speech was powerful and stirring. "We are tired of being at the bottom," he told the cheering crowd. "We are tired of working our hands off and laboring every day and not even making a wage adequate with the daily basic necessities of life."[3] As the theme of "we are tired," continued, the people were energized. Their feelings of hopelessness gave rise to a new enthusiasm. King had planned to make his short speech in Memphis and then get on with his schedule in other places. But he was so moved by the gratitude of the people that he decided to return to Memphis in ten days to personally lead the protest march on behalf of the striking workers.

The march was set for Thursday, March 28. King helped plan for the event. The black people of Memphis were encouraged to boycott their jobs that day. Black students were urged to stay out of school. The entire black community of Memphis was asked to support the sanitation workers.

Martin Luther King and Reverend Ralph Abernathy led the march, but disaster struck almost immediately. Some angry black youths began shouting Black Power slogans and smashing store windows along the march line. The police moved in with riot gear. King and Abernathy left the march. King explained, "I will never lead a violent march."[4]

King was brokenhearted about what had happened. In the thirteen years that he had led nonviolent marches all across the South, nothing like this had ever happened. By the next day King had resolved the problem in his mind. He believed he could have talked the violent youths out of their actions if he had known ahead of time what they had planned. He promised to return to Memphis in a week and vowed that the next demonstration would be nonviolent.

On April 3, King arrived in Memphis in good spirits. President Johnson had announced that he would not run for reelection in 1968, and King hoped this would hasten the end of the Vietnam War. Though suffering from a sore throat, King went out in a rainstorm to speak to a crowd at the Masonic Temple. His reception was so loud that it blocked out the thunder of the storm outside.

Martin Luther King delivered one of the most moving and passionate speeches of his life. "I've Been to the Mountaintop," he said. He pleaded for a nonviolent march on April 5. He recalled the civil rights struggles of the past and told the crowd: 'I've seen the promised land. I may not get there with you. But I want you to know tonight that we as a people will get to the promised land."[5]

On the morning of April 4, King met with his staff about the march set for the following day. The judge had lifted an injunction against the march, so it would be a legal protest. King's brother, A.D., was with him and they called their mother in Atlanta. King met with some black youths who had gang connections, and he pleaded with them to turn from violence.

At 6:00 P.M. King and Abernathy were getting ready to leave their room at the Lorraine Motel and go out to dinner. King stepped out on the iron balcony to talk to some

King on the balcony of the Lorraine Motel on April 3, 1968,
the day before he was assassinated there. From left: Hosea Williams,
Jesse Jackson, King, and Ralph Abernathy.

people in the courtyard below, including a musician he
knew. "Ben," King called, "I want you to sing for me
tonight. I want you to do that song 'Precious Lord.' Sing
it real pretty."[6]

Seconds later, a bullet, apparently from the direction
of a rooming house across the street, hit King in his lower
right jaw. The single 30.06-caliber bullet smashed his jaw-
bone, then pierced his neck, ripping open major blood

vessels and nerves. It severed his spinal cord before lodging in his shoulder blade.

Ralph Abernathy was close by when King was struck. He recalled later, "I looked down at Martin's face. His eyes wobbled." Abernathy knelt beside his friend and said, "Martin, it's all right. Don't worry. This is Ralph. This is Ralph."[7] The force of the bullet had hurled King backward. He lay on the balcony floor, his feet sticking through the railing. Abernathy pressed a towel to the terrible wound in an effort to stop the rapid bleeding. The bullet had removed the right side of King's jaw, and his head lay in a pool of blood. Abernathy and some others put a pillow under King's head as the frantic call for help went out.

When the ambulance arrived, paramedics rushed King to St. Joseph's Hospital. Abernathy rode in the ambulance and helped the paramedics check King's faint pulse and give him oxygen. King was taken to the emergency room at the hospital.

There was no time to remove King's clothing. A team of doctors and nurses cut the shirt and coat from his body and massaged his heart. The medical team worked frantically, but King could not be saved.

The hole in King's jaw was large enough to put two fists in it. The neurosurgeon in charge of the effort to save King's life told Abernathy, "I'm afraid it's over." At 7:05 P.M.,

April 4, 1968, the head physician said, "I'm sorry, but we've lost him. It's all over."[8]

Abernathy collected King's belongings, including his wallet and checkbook. Then he and other friends who had gathered at the hospital hugged one another and left.

Martin Luther King's parents in Atlanta heard the news of their son's death on the radio. Daddy King cried, "My first son, whose birth had brought me such joy that I jumped up in the hall outside the room where he was born and touched the ceiling—the child, the scholar, the preacher . . . all of it was gone."[9]

Coretta King had just returned from a shopping trip with her children when she received a phone call from family friend Jesse Jackson. He told her that her husband had been shot and that she should come to Memphis as quickly as possible. He did not tell her that King was dead.

The Kings' eldest child, Yolanda, was watching television when the news bulletin came on, announcing her father's death. The girl screamed.

Coretta King rushed to the Atlanta airport to take a flight to Memphis. When she reached the airport, she was escorted into a private room, where the mayor of Atlanta was waiting for her. He told her that her husband had died of the wounds he suffered. Coretta King now had no reason to hurry. She had four children at home who needed her desperately. She returned to the family home, where she found Yolanda praying behind the living room curtain,

"Lord, please take care of my mommy and make her strong."[10] Coretta comforted her daughter. She told the child not to hate the person who killed her father. Yolanda said she was not going to cry because "My daddy's not really dead, and I'm going to see him again in heaven."[11]

President Lyndon Johnson declared April 7 a day of national mourning for King. Johnson said he was "shocked and saddened" by the assassination, and then he added, "I ask every citizen to reject the blind violence that has struck Dr. King, who lived by nonviolence."[12]

Coretta King and her three older children went to Memphis on April 8 to take part in a memorial march honoring the part King had played in the just resolution of the Memphis sanitation workers strike. All the demands of the workers had been quickly agreed to by the city of Memphis.

"If a man hasn't discovered something that he will die for, he isn't fit to live."[13]

King's body was returned to Atlanta, where he lay in state in Sisters Chapel at Spelman College. Mourners came by the thousands. Each hour about twelve hundred people filed past the casket, pausing to honor the great leader. On April 9, eight hundred people gathered inside Ebenezer Baptist Church for the funeral service. A hundred thousand more heard the proceedings outside on loudspeakers. All the famous civil rights leaders of

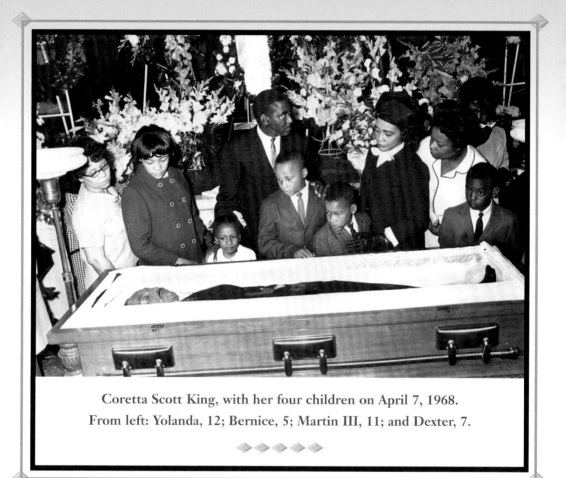

Coretta Scott King, with her four children on April 7, 1968.
From left: Yolanda, 12; Bernice, 5; Martin III, 11; and Dexter, 7.

the day, along with numerous celebrities, attended. Former attorney general Robert Kennedy and future president Richard Nixon joined Vice President Hubert Humphrey. Jacqueline Kennedy, widow of the assassinated president John F. Kennedy, mourned alongside King's many close friends.

The choir sang many of King's favorite hymns. Coretta King asked that the recording of a sermon King

The tomb of the great civil rights leader.

◆ ◆ ◆ ◆ ◆

had given at Ebenezer Church in February, titled "A Drum Major for Justice," be played at the funeral. In the sermon, King had responded to the question, "What would you like to be said on the day of your funeral?" He said, "Say that I was a drum major for peace. I was a drum major for righteousness."[14] When the Kings' youngest child, five-year-old Bernice, heard her father's voice, she turned her head around, searching for him.

Thousands walked in slow procession behind the special vehicle, called a poor person's hearse. It was a farm cart drawn by two mules. It carried King's body to South View Cemetery. The cemetery was blooming with dogwoods and fresh green boughs as King was laid to rest near the grave of his beloved grandmother Williams. On his tomb were the words "Free at last, free at last, thank God Almighty I'm free at last."

Chapter 10

The Legacy of the Dream

I n an outpouring of grief and anger following the assassination of Dr. Martin Luther King, Jr., rioting erupted in 125 American cities. Crowds of people smashed windows, and looted and burned stores. When the violence finally ended, there were forty-six dead and thirty-five thousand injured. Twenty thousand people had been arrested. President Johnson later said, "I remember the sick feeling that came over me . . . as I watched armed troops patrolling the streets [of Washington] . . . for the first time since the Civil War."[1]

The investigation into King's death began immediately, but it would be two months before the assassin was caught. An ex-convict named James Earl Ray was an early suspect after police found a bundle on the sidewalk near the Lorraine Motel. Inside was a Remington 30.06 Gamemaster rifle with a spent cartridge and ammunition. It belonged to Ray, whose fingerprints were on the rifle.

Two days after King was assassinated, terrible riots erupted in cities across the country—including Chicago, above.

Ray had been born in 1928 in Illinois. He was from a poor, working-class family. He learned to dislike African Americans from his father, who blamed them for many of society's problems.[2] Ray also learned bigotry from the frustrated poor whites in his neighborhood, who were looking for somebody to blame for their plight. As a child, Ray was a loner, frequently tormented by his peers for his dirty, ragged clothing and shyness. His teacher, writing an evaluation of the boy, described him as "repulsive."[3]

First arrested for stealing at age fourteen, Ray was

constantly in trouble for burglaries and armed robberies. During his many stays in prison, he allied with the white convicts against the blacks. He refused to participate in prison sports if African Americans were involved. He admired German dictator Adolf Hitler because he believed Hitler would make the United States an "all-white country, no Jews or Negroes."[4] He dreamed of moving to the British-ruled colony of Rhodesia in Africa, where the black majority was strictly segregated from the ruling whites.

Ray's entire life was one of bitterness, rejection, and failure. He confided in an acquaintance that he longed to be important enough someday to be on the FBI's Most Wanted list.[5]

Fifteen days after King's death, the FBI issued an all points bulletin for Ray. The evidence indicated that on April 4 he had posted himself in the window of a rooming house across from the Lorraine Motel, aiming at King, who was two hundred feet away. With the help of the seven-times magnification on the rifle's scope, King appeared only thirty feet away. Ray was able to place the crosshairs of the rifle's scope in the middle of King's head before he pulled the trigger. Then, when he saw King fall, he could have rushed to his Mustang and driven off. He fled first to Canada, then to London, England, where he was arrested in June 1968. At his trial in March 1969, Ray plead guilty to shooting Martin Luther King, Jr., and was sentenced to ninety-nine years in prison. Three days later, he withdrew his guilty plea, saying he had been forced to take the blame for the murder. For the next thirty years, until his death in prison in 1994, he claimed he was innocent of the crime. King's son, Dexter Scott King, was among those who believed in Ray's innocence. Conspiracy theories have been raised concerning the assassination of King, with accusations that the U.S. government was involved. There are those who dispute the conspiracy theory, and others who believe it is true.

One week after the death of Martin Luther King, Jr., the 1968 Civil Rights Act was passed. Called the Open Housing Act, it forbade any kind of housing discrimination in the United States. President Johnson immediately signed it into law.

A year after King's death, Coretta King announced her intention to develop the Martin Luther King, Jr., Center for Nonviolent Social Change in Atlanta. She devoted most of her time and energy in the following months and years to making this center a reality. The goal of the center was to promote Martin Luther King's values. Gifts, both large and small, poured into Atlanta for the center, and in 1979, construction began. In January 1982, the center was officially opened. There was a church, an exhibition center, meeting rooms, and a reflecting pool. King's body was brought from South View Cemetery and placed

The King Center for Nonviolent Social Change invited children from all over the country to paint a mural in tribute to the great leader.

in an elevated marble crypt at the Freedom Hall complex in the center.

Coretta King had four young children to raise alone, so the 1970s were very challenging for her. But she found time to bring the center into reality and also to campaign to make her husband's birthday a national holiday in America. This was finally accomplished in 1986, when President Ronald Reagan signed it into law.

During the 1970s, violent tragedy again struck the King family. Alberta King—Martin Luther King, Jr.'s mother—was playing the Lord's Prayer on the organ at Ebenezer Baptist Church in Atlanta on June 30, 1974, when a crazed man stood up in the congregation. He shot Alberta King to death, killed a deacon, and wounded another parishioner. The assassin, Marcus Wayne Chenault, was eventually sentenced to life in prison without parole.

In November 1984, Daddy King, the beloved pastor of Ebenezer Baptist Church from 1931 to 1975, and father of Martin Luther King, Jr., died of a heart attack at age eighty-four. In spite of the terrible toll violence had taken on him with the murders of his beloved son and wife, Daddy King had always refused to be overtaken by hatred.

At the culmination of the 1963 March on Washington for Jobs and Freedom, in the most memorable and stirring speech of his life, Dr. Martin Luther King, Jr., expressed his hopes for his own four little children. His death deprived those children of their father when the eldest, Yolanda, was twelve, and the youngest, Bernice, was five. But in the shadow of their father's towering legacy and with their mother's guidance, the four children have grown into successful adults.

Yolanda King earned a degree in acting from New York University. She has appeared in movies including *Ghosts of Mississippi* and the 1979 television miniseries

King. In 1999 she played a teacher in *Selma, Lord, Selma.* In 2004, Yolanda King wrote a book, *Open My Eyes, Open My Soul,* an inspirational collection of stories showing the triumph of the human spirit. When her father's birthday became a national holiday, she said, "I'd rather take daddy out to dinner than celebrate this holiday." Though she still misses her father, she has said, "I know he's very pleased with what I've done."[6]

Dexter King moved to California to pursue a career in film after writing his autobiography, *Growing Up King: An Intimate Memoir.* Seven years old when his father was killed, Dexter finds it difficult to talk about his father's death. He always says, "when my father left."[7] Until 2004, Dexter served as chairman and president of the King Center and acted as the family spokesperson. He is proud of the center's work to encourage "all people of goodwill to make the world a better place to live so that all people have the same rights and privileges."[8]

Martin Luther King, III, a successful motivational speaker, became president of the King Center at the start of 2005. Before that, he served as president of the Southern Christian Leadership Conference (SCLC).

The youngest of the King children, Bernice, wrote a book of sermons and speeches, *Hard Questions, Hard Answers.* She majored in psychology at Spelman College and received degrees in law and theology from Emory University. She alone of the four children followed their

The Man Inside the Hero

Reflecting on her father in 2004, Yolanda King said that when she sees pictures of him on television she feels awe, but the solemn great man giving powerful sermons is not the father she remembers. She recalled instead the daddy who was "full of love and laughter." She recalled him in the kitchen, dipping into the pots her mother was cooking. Yolanda's mother would say, "Stop, Martin. You're setting a bad example for the kids." But when her back was turned, he would go right back to dipping.[9]

father into the ministry. Her preaching often reminds the congregation of her father's speaking style.[10]

In the aftermath of Martin Luther King, Jr.'s death, there were hundreds of tributes. Cities all over America named streets, schools, and public buildings in his honor. His legacy has been widespread. By exposing injustices against African Americans, he led the way for other minorities to begin campaigning in their own interests. His courageous work inspired many members of the clergy to become advocates of the poor and marginalized.

Because of the civil rights movement, African Americans in the South gained equal access to public services and facilities. Before King started his marches, African Americans sat in the backs of buses and theaters, could not receive service in restaurants, and were often denied access to housing and good jobs. Their children attended inferior schools, and they were often denied the right to vote.

In May 2003, a series of public service ads were broadcast on radio and television illustrating the difference King had made. The ads asked this simple question— "What would the world be like if Martin Luther King, Jr.,

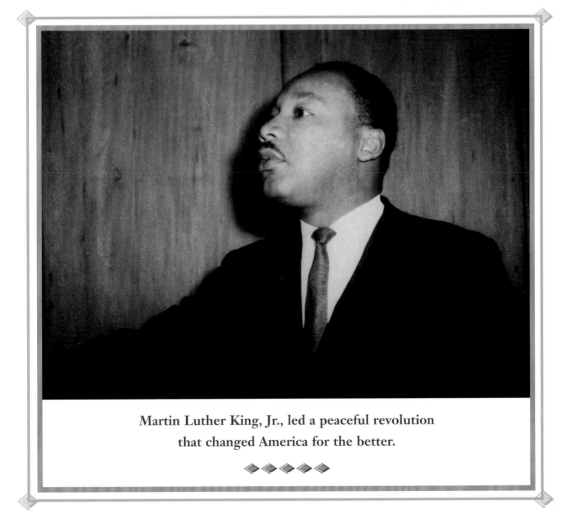

Martin Luther King, Jr., led a peaceful revolution
that changed America for the better.

never had a dream?" Actress Halle Berry and television personality Al Roker dramatized incidents of discrimination, such as a black customer entering a restaurant and being ushered to the rear "colored section."[11] For many, especially young people who never experienced segregation, these ads show how King transformed America.

King's work to bring down white supremacy in the South was a great victory for human freedom. King used his mastery of the spoken word to arouse African Americans to march behind his banner of nonviolent protest. He allowed himself to be jailed twenty-nine times, to be beaten, spat on, humiliated, and ridiculed. Had he resorted to violence in his crusade for equality for black people, America could have been plunged into a horrifying race war. By appealing to the best in people, he led a peaceful revolution that changed America for the better.

Martin Luther King, Jr., spoke of the triple evils of racism, poverty, and war. He showed how these could be constantly confronted, but he did not conquer any of them. The struggle against these evils continues, and it remains for all Americans to carry the banner he once did.

Chronology

1929—Martin Luther King, Jr., born in Atlanta, Georgia on January 15.

1944—Skips final year of high school to attend Morehouse College in Atlanta.

1948—Graduates from Morehouse College with a bachelor's degree in sociology; becomes associate pastor at Ebenezer Baptist Church in Atlanta, Georgia.

1951—Graduates from Crozer Theological Seminary in Chester, Pennsylvania, with a bachelor of divinity degree.

1953—Marries Coretta Scott on June 18.

1954—Becomes pastor of Dexter Avenue Baptist Church in Montgomery, Alabama.

1955—Receives doctorate in divinity from Boston University; first child, Yolanda Denise, born in November; becomes president of Montgomery Improvement Association (MIA) and leads a boycott of the segregated city bus system.

1957—Founds and becomes president of the Southern Christian Leadership Conference (SCLC); second child, Martin Luther King, III, born in October; receives Spingarn Medal.

1958—First book, *Stride Toward Freedom: The Montgomery Story*, published; stabbed in Harlem by deranged woman.

1959—Visits India and learns more about Gandhi techniques of nonviolence.

1960—Family moves to Atlanta, where King becomes co-pastor, with his father, of Ebenezer Baptist Church; supports formation of the Student Nonviolent Coordinating Committee (SNCC), an organization for student protests; meets with President Kennedy about racial issues; is arrested on charges of violating probation over a traffic charge.

1961—Third child, Dexter, born in January; supports Freedom Riders; leads march of segregation protesters in Albany Movement.

1963—Fourth child, Bernice Albertine, born in March; second book, *Strength to Love*, published; is arrested at demonstration against segregated lunch counters; "Letter from Birmingham Jail" is written from prison cell; delivers his "I Have a Dream" speech in Washington, D.C.

1964—Book *Why We Can't Wait*, is published; King is awarded the Nobel Peace Prize.

1965—Leads demonstrators for voting rights on a march from Selma to Montgomery, Alabama.

1966—Moves his family to a rented apartment in the poor section of Chicago to launch campaign for better housing.

CHRONOLOGY

1967—Publicly opposes Vietnam War; writes book *Where Do We Go From Here: Chaos or Community?*; helps plan Memphis March on behalf of striking sanitation and sewer workers.

1968—Delivers last speech, "I've Been to the Mountaintop," in Memphis, Tennessee; assassinated in Memphis on April 4.

1986—King's birthday is first celebrated as a federal holiday.

Chapter Notes

Chapter 1. "I've Had Enough"

    1. Stephen S. Oates, *Let the Trumpet Sound: The Life of Martin Luther King, Jr.* (New York: Harper and Row, 1982), p. 134.

    2. Ibid.

    3. William Roger Witherspoon, *Martin Luther King: To the Mountaintop* (New York: Doubleday, 1985), p. 60.

    4. Ibid.

    5. Oates, p. 136.

Chapter 2. "The Perfect Child"

    1. Clayborne Carson, ed., *The Autobiography of Martin Luther King, Jr.* (New York: Warner Books, 1998), p. 2.

    2. Stephen S. Oates, *Let the Trumpet Sound: The Life of Martin Luther King, Jr.* (New York: Harper and Row, 1982), p. 5.

    3. David J. Garrow, *Bearing the Cross: Martin Luther King, Jr., and the Southern Christian Leadership Conference* (New York: William Morrow, 1986), p. 33.

    4. Adam Fairclough, *Martin Luther King, Jr.* (Athens, Georgia: University of Georgia Press, 1995), p. 6.

    5. Carson, p. 4.

    6. Garrow, p. 34.

    7. Martin Luther King, Jr., *Stride Toward Freedom: The Montgomery Story* (New York: Harper and Brothers, 1958), p. 20.

8. Stephen B. Oates, *Let the Trumpet Sound: The Life of Martin Luther King, Jr.* (New York: Harper and Row, 1982), pp. 9–10.

9. Garrow, p. 33.

10. Ibid., p. 38.

11. King, p. 19.

12. Carson, p. 7.

13. Garrow, p. 35.

14. Oates, p. 17.

15. Carson, p. 11.

Chapter 3. Minister and Husband

1. William Roger Witherspoon, *Martin Luther King: To the Mountaintop* (New York: Doubleday, 1985), p. 5.

2. Stephen B. Oates, *Let the Trumpet Sound: The Life of Martin Luther King, Jr.* (New York: Harper and Row, 1982), p. 20.

3. Ibid.

4. David J. Garrow, *Bearing the Cross: Martin Luther King, Jr., and the Southern Christian Leadership Conference* (New York: William Morrow, 1986), p. 40.

5. Witherspoon, p. 8.

6. Ibid.

7. Ibid., pp. 10–11.

8. Clayborne Carson, ed., *The Autobiography of Martin Luther King, Jr.* (New York: Warner Books, 1998), p. 31.

9. Ibid., p. 34.

10. Oates, p. 42.

11. Carson, pp. 34–35.

12. Ibid., p. 35.

13. Oates, p. 43.

14. Garrow, p. 45.

15. Oates, p. 43.

16. Ibid.

17. Witherspoon, p. 13.

18. Oates, p. 45.

19. Ibid., p. 51.

Chapter 4. The Responsibility of Leadership

1. Clayborne Carson, ed., *The Autobiography of Martin Luther King, Jr.* (New York: Warner Books, 1998), p. 49.

2. Martin Luther King, Jr., *Stride Toward Freedom: The Montgomery Story* (New York: Harper and Brothers, 1958), p. 53.

3. Ibid., p. 63.

4. Adam Fairclough, *Martin Luther King, Jr.* (Athens, Georgia: University of Georgia Press, 1995), p. 24.

5. Ibid., p. 48.

6. William Roger Witherspoon, *Martin Luther King: To the Mountaintop* (New York: Doubleday, 1985), p. 36.

7. Ibid.

8. King, pp. 134–135.

9. Ibid., p. 137.

10. Witherspoon, p. 43.

11. King, p. 173.

12. Witherspoon, p. 52.

13. Ibid., p. 53.

14. Stephen B. Oates, *Let the Trumpet Sound: The Life of Martin Luther King, Jr.* (New York: Harper and Row, 1982), p. 125.

15. Ibid., p. 134.

16. Ibid., p. 138.

17. Charles Johnson and Bob Adelman, *King: The Photobiography of Martin Luther King, Jr.* (New York: Viking, 2000), p. 55.

18. Ibid.

19. Witherspoon, p. 61.

20. Oates, p. 143.

21. Carson, p. 129.

22. Oates, p. 146.

Chapter 5. The Fight for Freedom

1. Stephen B. Oates, *Let the Trumpet Sound: The Life of Martin Luther King, Jr.* (New York: Harper and Row, 1982), p. 152.

2. William Roger Witherspoon, *Martin Luther King: To the Mountaintop* (New York: Doubleday, 1985), p. 71.

3. Oates, p. 152.

4. Ibid., p. 155.

5. Ibid., p. 156.

6. Witherspoon, p. 74.

7. Oates, p. 163.

8. Adam Fairclough, *Martin Luther King, Jr.* (Athens, Georgia: University of Georgia Press, 1996), p. 67.

9. Witherspoon, p. 107.

Chapter 6. Birmingham

1. Donald T. Phillips, *Martin Luther King, Jr., on Leadership* (New York: Warner Books, 1999), p. 155.

2. Adam Fairclough, *Martin Luther King, Jr.* (Athens, Georgia: University of Georgia Press, 1995), p. 77.

3. Ibid.

4. William Roger Witherspoon, *Martin Luther King: To the Mountaintop* (New York: Doubleday, 1985), p. 121.

5. Martin Luther King, Jr., *The Words of Martin Luther King, Jr.* (New York: Pocket Books, 1983), p. 38.

6. Phillips, p. 169.

7. Ibid., p. 170.

8. Fairclough, p. 85.

9. Witherspoon, p. 135.

Chapter 7. "I Have a Dream"

1. Martin Luther King, Jr., *The Words of Martin Luther King, Jr.* (New York: Pocket Books, 1983), p. 83.

2. Ibid., pp. 85–86.

3. William Roger Witherspoon, *Martin Luther King: To the Mountaintop* (New York: Doubleday, 1985), p. 144.

4. Stephen B. Oates, *Let the Trumpet Sound: The Life of Martin Luther King, Jr.* (New York: Harper and Row, 1982), p. 267.

5. Witherspoon, p. 149.

6. Donald T. Phillips, *Martin Luther King, Jr., on Leadership* (New York: Warner Books, 1999), p. 174.

7. Oates, p. 281.

8. Ibid.

9. Oates, p. 283.

10. Ibid.

11. Witherspoon, p. 150.

12. Phillips, p. 310.

13. Witherspoon, p. 150.

14. Phillips, p. 181.

15. Ibid., p. 277.

CHAPTER NOTES

Chapter 8. Nobel Prize and Vietnam

1. William Roger Witherspoon, *Martin Luther King: To the Mountaintop* (New York: Doubleday, 1985), p. 167.

2. Ibid.

3. Adam Fairclough, *Martin Luther King, Jr.* (Athens, Georgia: University of Georgia Press, 1995), p. 99.

4. David J. Garrow, *Bearing the Cross: Martin Luther King, Jr., and the Southern Christian Leadership Conference* (New York: William Morrow, 1986), p. 373.

5. Stephen B. Oates, *Let the Trumpet Sound: The Life of Martin Luther King, Jr.* (New York: Harper and Row, 1982), p. 332.

6. Garrow, p. 374.

7. Oates, p. 333.

8. Ibid., p. 334.

9. Witherspoon, p. 181.

10. Garrow, p. 543.

11. Charles Johnson and Bob Adelman, *King: The Photobiography of Martin Luther King, Jr.* (New York: Viking, 2000), p. 234.

12. Donald T. Phillips, *Martin Luther King, Jr., on Leadership* (New York: Warner Books, 1999), p. 294.

13. Ibid., p. 295.

14. Witherspoon, p. 210.

15. Clayborne Carson, ed., *The Autobiography of Martin Luther King, Jr.* (New York: Warner Books, 1998), p. 342.

16. Ibid., p. 345.

Chapter 9. "Free at Last"

1. Gerald Posner, *Killing the Dream: James Earl Ray and the Assassination of Martin Luther King, Jr.* (New York: Random House, 1998), p. 3.

2. Donald T. Phillips, *Martin Luther King, Jr., on Leadership* (New York: Warner Books, 1999), pp. 322–323.

3. Ibid., p. 323.

4. Ibid.

5. Martin Luther King, Jr., *The Words of Martin Luther King, Jr.* (New York: Pocket Books, 1983), p. 80.

6. Posner, p. 30.

7. Ibid.

8. Stephen B. Oates, *Let the Trumpet Sound: The Life of Martin Luther King, Jr.* (New York: Harper and Row, 1982), p. 491.

9. Ibid., p. 493.

10. William Roger Witherspoon, *Martin Luther King: To the Mountaintop* (New York: Doubleday, 1985), p. 223.

11. Ibid.

12. Associated Press, *Los Angeles Times*, April 5, 1968, p. 1.

13. Charles Johnson and Bob Adelman, *King: Photobiography of Martin Luther King, Jr.* (New York: Viking, 2000), p. 285.

14. Witherspoon, p. 225.

Chapter 10. The Legacy of the Dream

1. Adam Fairclough, *Martin Luther King, Jr.* (Athens, Georgia: University of Georgia Press, 1995), p. 124.

CHAPTER NOTES

2. Gerald Posner, *Killing the Dream: James Earl Ray and the Assassination of Martin Luther King, Jr.* (New York: Random House, 1998), p. 332.

3. Ibid., p. 83.

4. Ibid., p. 91.

5. Ibid., p. 212.

6. "Marching On," *People Weekly*, January 18, 1999, p. 59.

7. Joy Bennett Kinnon, "Dexter King Confronts His Critics and Reveals His Dreams," *Ebony*, January 2003, p. 122.

8. Ibid.

9. Karen M. Thomas, "Martin Luther King's Eldest Daughter Finds Her Own Way," *San Diego Union*, April 22, 2004, p. E3.

10. Kim Hubbard, "Dreamgirl: Bernice King, Martin Luther's Youngest Child, Has Grown Up to Be the Guardian of His Legacy," *People Weekly*, January 27, 1997, p. 76.

11. *U.S. Newswire*, "New PSA Campaign Featuring Halle Berry and Al Roker Examines 'What the World Would be Like If Martin Luther King, Jr. Never Had a Dream,'" May 7, 2003.

Further Reading

Ganeri, Anita, and Nicola Barber. *Martin Luther King, Jr.* Chicago: Raintree, 2003.

Haskins, James. *The Life and Words of Martin Luther King, Jr.* Brookfield, Conn.: Millbrook, 1993.

King, Martin Luther, Jr. *I Have a Dream: Writings and Speeches That Changed the World.* San Francisco: HarperCollins, 1992.

Manheimer, Ann S. *Martin Luther King, Jr.: Dreaming of Equality.* Minneapolis: Carolrhoda Books, 2005.

Pastan, Amy. *Martin Luther King, Jr.* New York: DK Publishing, 2004.

Wukovits, John F. *Martin Luther King, Jr.* San Diego, Calif.: Lucent Books, 1999.

Internet Addresses

The story of the Selma march of 1965.
  <http://www.msnbc.com/onair/modules/
    selma.asp?cp1=1>

Audio and video on King Center, his life and works.
  <http://thekingcenter.org/tkc/index.asp>

**Interactive audio and video on King's life. Many
excellent photos.**
  <http://www.stanford.edu/group/King/>

Index

Page numbers for photographs are in **boldface** type.